PRAISE FOR
WILD WEST GHOSTS

As a weathered investigator of the strange, as well as a road-weary traveler, I'm always thrilled when someone reveals exciting and unusual locations I can add to my journeys. Mark and Kym have succeeded in creating a wonderfully weird travel guide for both veteran and novice paranormal enthusiasts. We live in a mysterious world filled with peculiar happenings, and Mark and Kym have done a fantastic job illuminating some of the curious corners of our world so that all of us may see them. This book is a wonderful addition to any library but keep it in your travel-bag, not on the shelf.

John E.L. Tenney
Co-host of Destination America's
Ghost Stalkers television series

❧

Get your bags packed! Once you read *Wild West Ghosts*, you will be ready to hop a train to Colorado and meet these spirits yourself! *Wild West Ghosts* is a splendidly written excursion into southwest Colorado's haunted hotels. Kym and Mark not only fill you in on the history of the hotels and the area, but also efficiently communicate the atmosphere of each location, from the wisps of cigar smoke in a hallway to the sound of spurs as forgotten cowboys walk. These are not "ghost stories" but rather a collection of documented paranormal evidence that they collected at each of these wonderful Colorado hotels from the past. Comprised of eyewitness testimonies, historical accounts, and their own terrifying time spent in these historical hotels, *Wild West Ghosts* is your tour guide to a wild ride of haunted locations that will definitely keep you from getting a good night's sleep!

Shane & Jennifer Herrin
Founders of **Small Town Haunts**

There are as many books written about ghosts and ghost hunting as there are skeptics behind them. Mark and Kym, once skeptics themselves, have transformed this paranormal literary genre, bringing it to a whole new level. In their captivating book and travel companion, *Wild West Ghosts*, a reader will step back in time to experience the Old West in a new light through the many supernatural legends and histories tied to the Rocky Mountain area. Inside you will journey with them as you experience, first-hand, entities interacting through EVP recorders, EMF detectors, and spirit boxes. Mark and Kym's paranormal team focuses on guiding both ghost hunting veterans and novices through their experiences inside the myriad of lavish period hotels and bed and breakfasts scattered throughout the Colorado area. Their investigations are performed not at night, like nearly every other paranormal team, but in the daytime. And the results are amazing!

The team is graciously welcomed to each site by its innkeepers and every visit has its own unique story to tell. One of my favorites lies in the town of Cripple Creek. Here a man attempts to dynamite a Sisters of Mercy hospital kitchen, only to have his leg blown off: "His shoe, which had landed in the tea kettle, was kept by the Sisters as a memento." Events like these resonate throughout the book and lay the foundation for great paranormal activity.

Wild West Ghosts is a must-read not only for those passionate about the paranormal world but also for Old West history buffs or anyone who loves to travel and experience a wonderful overnight stay. The coolest part of all is that they provide very specific local information, much like a travel guide, that will allow you the opportunity to find each of these beautiful locations and to do your own ghost hunting…and perhaps experience the very same paranormal events!

– Timothy Yohe, paranormal investigator
and founder of **Paranormal Insights**

Also by Kym O'Connell-Todd and Mark Todd

The Silverville Swindle
(Ghost Road Press)

The Silverville Saga
Little Greed Men
All Plucked Up
The Magicke Outhouse
(Raspberry Creek Books)

By Mark Todd

Wire Song
(Conundrum Press)

Tamped, But Loose Enough to Breathe
(Ghost Road Press)

Strange Attractors
(Write in the Thick)

WILD WEST GHOSTS
an amateur ghost hunting guide for
HAUNTED HOTELS
in southwest Colorado

Mark Todd
&
Kym O'Connell-Todd

RASPBERRY
CREEK

BOOKS

WILD WEST GHOSTS: An Amateur Ghost Hunting Guide
For Haunted Hotels in Southwest Colorado

Copyright © 2015 by Mark Todd and Kym O'Connell-Todd

All rights reserved. In accordance with the U.S. Copyright Act of 1976, the scanning, uploading, and electronic sharing of any part of this book without the permission of the publisher constitute unlawful piracy and theft of the author's intellectual property. If you would like to use material from the book (other than for review purposes), prior written permission must be obtained by contacting the publisher at info@raspberrycreekbooks.com. Thank you for your support of the author's rights.

ISBN: 978-0-9851352-6-3
Library of Congress Control Number: 2015939292

Printed in the United States of America

www.raspberrycreekbooks.com

Raspberry Creek Books, Ltd.
Gunnison, CO   Tulsa, OK

Cover Design by: Write in the Thick

For all the lingering tenants
at the establishments we visited.

ACKNOWLEDGEMENTS

We wish to recognize all the people who helped bring this book to publication. Thank you to the owners of all the hotels, inns, and B&Bs who allowed us to investigate their establishments and the staff who consented to interviews and guided us to ghostly hotspots. Thank you, Teresa Milbrodt and Marty Grantham for the careful line edits and constructive criticism. And thanks to long-time paranormal investigator Debra Anderson for vetting the methodology we propose for readers of this book.

We want to thank Wraiths in the Thick of Things investigative team members Moonbeam Aboc, Fonda Porterfield, and Egan Kelso, who each assisted during ghost investigations conducted for various chapters. Hotchkiss Paranormal Investigators as well as Shaun Crusha helped strengthen the integrity of our procedures, and paranormal professional Mark Ashby, moderator for London's @HauntedHour, encouraged and gave us pointers – to all of whom we are grateful. We also acknowledge Toni Tuttle for her "insightful" contributions to an experiment in one of our investigations.

More special thanks go to Shane and Jennifer Herrin, founders of Small Town Haunts; John E.L. Tenney, co-host of Destination America's *Ghost Stalkers*; and Timothy Yohe, founder and author of *Paranormal Insights* – all were kind enough to read our manuscript and offer us valuable comments about the content.

And finally, our thanks to our publisher, Larry Meredith of Raspberry Creek Books, who encouraged us over drinks to embark on this project and who published this book.

Table of Contents

Introduction

1. **Creede**
   - Creede Hotel — *p. 19*
2. **Crested Butte**
   - Forest Queen Hotel — *p. 35*
3. **Cripple Creek**
   - Hotel St. Nicholas — *p. 49*
   - Linda Goodman's Miracle Inn/Last Dollar Inn B&B — *p. 62*
4. **Del Norte**
   - Windsor Hotel — *p. 75*
5. **Delta**
   - Fairlamb House B&B — *p. 89*
6. **Fairplay**
   - Fairplay Hotel — *p. 105*
   - Hand Hotel — *p. 118*
7. **Gunnison**
   - Vintage Inn — *p. 131*
8. **Norwood**
   - Hotel Norwood — *p. 147*
9. **Ouray**
   - Beaumont Hotel & Spa — p. 161
10. **Paonia**
    - Bross Hotel — *p. 175*
11. **South Fork**
    - Spruce Lodge — *p. 189*
12. **Twin Lakes**
    - Twin Lakes Inn — p. 203
13. **When You Get Back Home** — *p. 217*
14. *Afterword* — *p. 231*

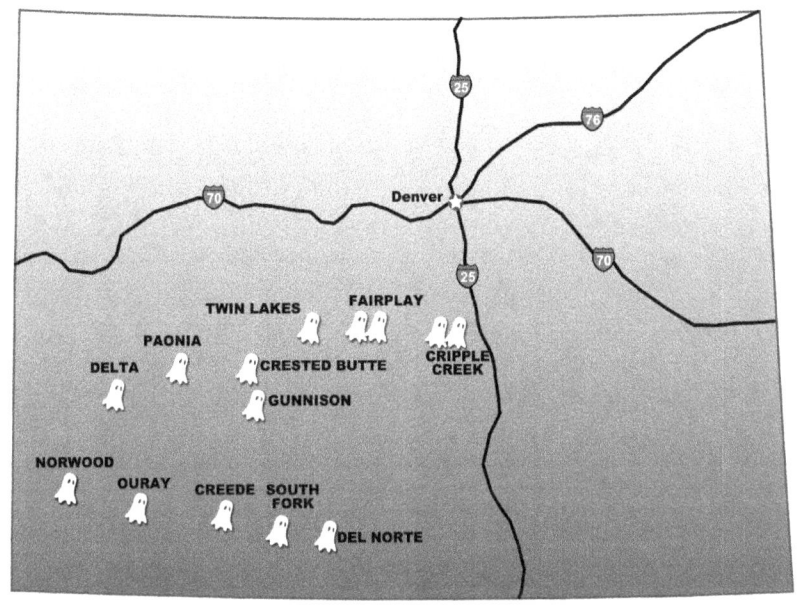

*The Locations of the
Haunted Hotels
We Visited for This Book*

INTRODUCTION

"The vast majority of us don't like the idea of our own mortality. Even though we find the idea of ghosts and spirits scary, in a wider context, they provide evidence for the survival of the soul."

— Christopher French, professor of psychology and head of the Anomalistic Psychology Research Unit at Goldsmiths, University of London
(*The Atlantic* Sept. 2014)

WHY WE WROTE THIS BOOK

Do we as authors believe in ghosts? Kinda, not at first, maybe, sometimes. So where do we fall in the 2013 Harris Poll? Here's the run-down of believers in the United States:

- God: 74 percent
- The Devil: 58 percent
- Darwin's Theory of Evolution: 47 percent
- Ghosts: 42 percent
- Creationism and UFOs: 36 percent each
- Astrology: 29 percent
- Witches: 26 percent
- Reincarnation: 24 percent

Fear not. With that said, we don't intend to bore the pants off you by analyzing assorted anthropological and psychological studies. This isn't that sort of book. For the 42 percent of you ghost believers, this book will reaffirm what you've thought all along. For the 58 percent of you nonbelievers, we hope this book will open up possibilities.

For all of you, these chapters will serve as a fun theme vacation guide to haunted hotels across mountainous southwestern Colorado.

Okay, back to us. Neither of us really believed in ghosts for much of our adult lives. We found ourselves amused at all the reality ghost shows, we snickered at our friends' anecdotes, and we agreed with skeptics who explained away all the really cool things people wanted to believe.

Then we moved into a haunted house for nine years. That changed everything.

The "haunted house" where we lived for nine years

We'd rented a 900-square-foot, two-story log cabin, which sat on ground that was the first site occupied by the frontier mining and ranching community of Doyleville, Colorado. The only remaining evidence of that settlement are a few foundations, the original stage stop (now a storage shed), and the berm that supported the 1800s narrow-gauge railroad tracks.

A hundred years ago, most of the bustling little "town" of 2,000 residents consisted of haphazard assemblies of tents with occasional wooden false storefronts for local commerce. These days, Doyleville is a ranching community of around three dozen families scattered over a hundred square miles.

Our family of two adults and two little girls occupied the cozy two-bedroom cabin, which had a two-flight stairway divided by a landing. It wasn't until one night, when Kym asked Mark to go downstairs for a soda pop from the fridge and learned he didn't want to go down the stairwell. That small request started a discussion about how we both sensed that spot in the house was, well ... creepy. In fact, we both had noticed it since we'd moved in but felt too silly to mention the feeling to each other.

We shrugged it off, even laughed about our separate if coincidental impressions. But then our girls mentioned they didn't like to go to the bathroom down that hall in the middle of the night because it felt uncomfortable. Several years later they admitted they'd each seen a man dressed in old-time clothes in the hallway near the stairwell, an experience they hadn't even shared with each other at the time.

After a couple of years living in the cabin, a neighbor mentioned that the first burial was on our place – an unmarked grave. That seemed a bit much for a coincidence.

On two occasions, different friends came to visit (each later confessed they were "sensitive" to paranormal phenomena) and each told us there was a presence in the stairwell. One of these friends refused to come inside the cabin. In both instances, we hadn't previously discussed our "in-house" secret with them.

It was time to clear the air, in a manner of speaking. So one evening we sat in the stairwell and had a little chat with our extra resident, suggesting we all try to get along since we were all, ahem, *living* under the same roof. That conversation seemed to do the trick. We felt better about it, and neither of us minded going down the stairs after that.

Did the feeling of a presence go away? No. It just felt less creepy. And by then we quit worrying about the pranks that continued to happen – lights going on and off, the satellite TV changing channels without our directions, the sound of our piano playing in the middle of the night, the water facets turning on and off. (Did we mention the cabin wasn't old? It was built as a summer retreat just a few years prior and turned into a rental. There was no old and creaky plumbing, etc.)

One of the oddest things occurred when we returned from a three-day trip. Our downstairs had a half-bath/laundry room: just a shallow sink, a toilet, and a washer/dryer. We kept the cat box on the far side of the dryer and well away from the sink, and Kym checked the box (full of soiled litter, of course) and went to get a garbage bag. When she returned half a minute later, she found the cat box full of water. The box was too large to fit under the little sink as a prank. Besides, no one could have done the deed in so short a time, and we were all too exhausted from a fourteen-hour drive.

Cute trick, Mr. Ghost.

Eventually, the girls grew up and we needed more than two bedrooms so we moved, not once mentioning our extra resident to the landlord.

We later learned that the next two consecutive tenants lasted only six months each, and both complained that the cabin was haunted. One even walked away from a lease and had to keep paying *not* to live there. In neither case had either of the tenants heard about the resident ghost ahead of time.

Finally, the landlord retired and moved in. We heard his wife wouldn't stay there. A former neighbor recently told us the wife still prefers to stay in the primitive guest cabin with no electricity or plumbing right next door.

We moved out seventeen years ago, but the experience gave us an open mind. Or at least a greater level of tolerance for unannounced roommates.

In some ways, we're surprised it's taken us this long to bring our journalistic talents to bear on a book about ghosts.

But here we are now: researching, investigating, and writing about ghosts. Other people's ghosts.

Why We Chose These Hotels

We initially researched twenty-six candidates with paranormal reputations, narrowing our list to the fourteen hotels, inns, and B&Bs included in this book. By design, we discounted the more famous and larger city establishments and instead sought out smaller towns with a Wild West flavor, some a bit off the beaten track.

That doesn't mean these hotels lack creature comforts. Each one is an operating facility that offers a pleasant stay and expected amenities.

Equally important, we didn't want to send our readers into uncomfortable situations. It was our experience that all of the hotels listed here contain ghosts that seem merely mischievous rather than threatening. And Colorado splendor surrounds each and every hotel. After your ghostly encounters, you can take advantage of a wide array of nearby activities and recreational opportunities. (See the "Highlights" section at the end of each chapter.) All our featured accommodations fall within the southwestern Colorado region, making it possible to stay at several during a short vacation.

Filled with frontier history, these locations abound with tales of lawlessness, gunfights, brothels, and mining lore. We encourage you to research the bygone eras of your chosen destinations as a way to enrich your experiences.

The Equipment We Used

From the beginning, we decided to keep our equipment simple and use the same devices and resources we envisioned the bulk of our readers taking to the haunted hotels featured in this book.

For the most part, you can use apps that are easy to upload on your phone or tablet – even better, you can select from many that are free from sources such as GooglePlay or the Apple Store.

What do you need? Beginning on the next page we offer **a basic toolkit**, along with brief descriptions of each and a few tips that can make your ghost hunting enjoyable and successful.

Our own travel kit (cat optional)

- **Audio recording equipment**
  Most phones and tablets have this capability already, but you may want to add a separate device at the same time you're using other apps during an investigation. In this case, the goal as ghost hunters is to capture voices too faint to hear in real time but audible when amplified during later analysis; these recordings are known as EVPs (**E**lectronic **V**oice **P**henomena). A suitable digital recorder can be had anywhere from $20-$50. No need for anything more sophisticated.

- **Spirit box**
  This is an electronic device or else an app that scans radio frequencies, allowing spirits to select words off the airways as a way to communicate. Such devices are sometimes called ghost boxes. After we'd completed several of the investigations for this book, we added an EchoVox ($30), which generates random sounds (no words) and doesn't rely on radio wave frequencies. An alternative device generating random one-second sounds is Spotted:Ghost's Spirit Box (free). The advantage is not having to worry about weak or blocked signals in remote

or mountainous locations. Both are available for Android or iPhone users. If you have a Windows-based tablet, you might also consider a RIFF Ghost Box (also $30).

- **EMF meter**
  EMF stands for **E**lectro**m**agnetic **F**ield, and this device or app lets you observe and record fluctuations in EM field strengths – a common paranormal signal that ghosts are present or trying to communicate. Most such devices register milli-Gauss units (mG). One Gauss is about the strength of the magnetic field of the Earth, whereas paranormal activity tends to occur at a much subtler level, one-thousandth of a Gauss.

- **Still camera and video camera**
  Again, most phones and tablets provide sufficient capability to document what you experience. However, it's useful to have a separate device, so you don't have to interrupt the apps you're running at the same time.

- **Flashlight**
  Nothing fancy, but stronger is better. We used an over-the-counter 160-lumen flashlight we picked up at a convenience store. The stronger the light, the easier it is for ghosts to use that energy to communicate.

- **Extra batteries for all devices**
  Ghosts often draw on the energy of the devices you bring to an investigation as a way to make their presence known, so don't be surprised if you have to replace batteries often.

- **Notebook and pen**
  Always keep a log of what happens, so you can review and share your experiences. We encourage everyone in your group to write separate logs, which you can compare

afterward. A log also helps you keep a sequence of events straight – it's sometimes important to discover or recognize connections between recordings or measurements from different devices.

You'll also want to download **simple sound editing software** for your computer or laptop to enhance any audio recordings you make. For the investigations in this book we used Audacity software, which is the free kid sister to SoundForge's audio editing suite and allowed us to amplify or enhance audio recordings as well as turn them into .wav or .mp3 files. You might consider **earbuds** or **headphones** as well, so you can pick up more subtle words.

If you find yourself getting more ambitious, consider the following additions:

- **Camcorder and tripod**
  This allows for static placement, either to document your investigations or to observe locations in your absence. Our camcorder came with software that allows us to edit movies and create .mp4 files to upload documentation of our findings to YouTube. (In fact, we invite you to view our clips online. The direct URL to our EVPs and video recordings is youtube.com/c/KymnMarkTodd.)
- **External Bluetooth speaker**
  Never hurts to have a bit more amplification for your recordings.
- **Ambient air thermometer**
  Useful for measuring "cold spots" – regions or pockets of air where the temperature drops while ghosts convert energy in order to manifest or communicate.

Of course, other specialty equipment is available, such as infrared and thermal imaging cameras. Do you need them all? Not really. We got by fine with the basic toolkit and still came away with findings that made all our investigations both satisfying and productive. Keeping your toolkit simple has the added advantage of making you more mobile – not to mention it's easier to pack and unpack for travel!

Keep in mind that using electronic devices during investigations sometimes produces anomalies – after all, ghosts try to use the energy generated by those same devices as a means of communication. We occasionally assumed our equipment malfunctioned during an investigation when, in fact, it worked perfectly when we tested later at home.

A Proposed Investigation Methodology

You've assembled your equipment and arrived on site at a haunted hotel. Now what?

First, a suggestion: We've all seen the TV ghost shows, featuring nighttime "lock-downs" designed to create entertainment and goose bumps. In our opinion, it's just as valid – maybe more so – to conduct investigations in the daytime when your imagination isn't going into overdrive. Many guest and staff reports of apparitions included in this book occurred during daylight hours. We followed the advice of professional paranormal investigator Benjamin Radford and conducted all of our own investigations in daytime, so we could actually see something. We used this as a standard protocol to make our findings consistent.

And really, do ghosts care what time it is?

Following is a proposed investigation methodology:

- Start your investigation by taking lots of photos – even in spaces that don't look interesting. Be sure to keep a log that records the subject, location, date, and time of each image you capture.
- Take EMF readings throughout a room or location you intend to investigate in order to establish baseline electromagnetic field strengths, noting variations in different parts of the room. This gives you a foundation for comparison during the rest of your investigation. Then be sure to leave your EMF meter on while you conduct other experiments in case you get elevated readings.
- Set up your video camera to document your investigation. We always record our experiments. You might also consider pointing the camcorder in other areas of the room and at times when you're not present or awake.
- Turn on the camcorder, audio recorder, and spirit box before you ask questions.
- Introduce yourselves, tell the spirits why you're there, and ask them to communicate with you. Be polite. These *were* live humans at one time and deserve respect. You should also explain the function of your equipment and then request they respond to you through those instruments.
- Take notes of any real-time responses.
- Conduct a separate audio-only recording (you'll need to turn off your spirit box for this) to try capturing EVPs to your questions. It's important that the room is quiet – no running air conditioners or open windows that make noise and corrupt your results.

- Flip on your flashlight and ask the spirits to use that energy to communicate by flickering, dimming, or completely turning off the light. (Give them time; ghosts aren't trained dogs.)

Flashlight Session

During all the experiments, continue to check your EMF meter. On multiple occasions, our sessions produced high spikes on our meter at the same time we asked for communication or observed the flashlight dimming.

After the session – either later on site or back at home – comes the fun part of analyzing your findings for evidence you may have missed in real time. Watch your video recordings. Examine your photos for orbs, streaks of light, or any other anomaly. Don't dismiss seemingly failed photos. At one hotel Kym captured a series of pictures containing only streaks of color. We learned later that such photos are common in ghost investigations.

Download your audio files to your laptop or computer. Analyze your spirit box results with audio editing software (Audacity, for example, lets you manipulate portions of sound files by amplifying, slowing down, changing pitch, compressing noise, etc.) If you took audio-only recordings, you can also analyze your results on your editing software. We recommend you use earphones for this, so you can hear even faint voices.

Don't be surprised if different members of your investigative team come up with varying interpretations of EVP sounds, words, or phrases. (For the purposes of this book, we didn't include EVPs if we couldn't agree that we heard the same thing.) Be aware you may also record voices in another language – the hotels in this book began in locales teeming with miners from m many different countries.

The above investigative procedures use an approach known as Instrumental Trans-Communication (ITC) – using devices to contact spirits. But your own experiences may extend beyond gadgets. We don't consider ourselves "sensitives." Nonetheless, our personal encounters included events such as ghostly touches, cold spots, aromas, and sensations of unseen presences.

Our Ghost-Hunting Test-Drive (and Mistakes) In Virginia City, MT

We leave you with a cautionary tale. Read and learn.

Before we launched this project, we decided to test-drive our new ghost-hunting equipment while on vacation at notorious Virginia City, second capitol to Montana and home to 1800s vigilantes. The original buildings still fill the town and, according to some, ghosts still walk the streets.

Local law enforcement graciously allowed us to visit the courthouse, including the original old jail cells. We also investigated several other hotspots in this very haunted frontier mining town. Our team included two savvy locals, "Moonbeam Aboc" (not her real name) and Fonda Porterfield.

Following are highlights:

The Courthouse

*Virginia City Courthouse of late 1880s.
It has changed very little.*

Built in 1876, site of many hangings on the front steps, disturbed by earthquakes and major fires several times. Notable events in the investigation:

- Interviewed several deputies and dispatch staff, who recounted repeated paranormal activities, including footsteps, clanging and knocking, unexplained disruption of CTV during many of these events, and turned-over pews (all of them) in the courtroom during the middle of the night minutes after the janitor cleaned the room.

- Staked out the old jail, *still* in use as holding cells, and recorded several photos with clear orbs (a first for us), with spirit box confirmations describing our ongoing, on-site activity. (We captured the words "film," "videotape," and "floodlights," both when we turned on and turned off such lights, plus repeated references to "fire," burning," and "flame.")

The courthouse pews a janitor found overturned

Where an orb followed the jailer as she moved about

- Investigated the courtroom, where many reports of apparitions and footsteps occurred on the adjoining empty stairwell. (We recorded multiple spirit box confirmations of the words "stairwell" and "staircase.")
- Recorded baseline EMF readings in the 150-200mG range that spiked to 2,000mG (holding cells) and 4,000mG (courtroom) and then disappeared. Recorded readings that jumped three times higher (200mG up to 700mG) on approaching the courthouse steps where many hanging executions occurred.
- Captured two interesting EVPs, one a whispered voice that named "Moonbeam's" real name, and another unintelligible but clearly human voice in the holding cells.

The Hanging Building

This was the site of a multiple-lynching incident by the notorious Vigilantes of Montana in 1864.

- Team member "Moonbeam" snapped two cellphone pics back to back, first capturing two ghost "ropes" that dangled from the hanging beam, and the second photo taken moments later but revealing no such thing.

The Wells Fargo Steakhouse

Underneath the current premises was the original city morgue, where deceased individuals were stored in wintertime, pending enough ground thaw to bury. In the same basement staff have reported seeing and hearing the well-known, though enigmatic, ghost of "Angry Dan."

- Spirit box immediately announced "Daniel" as we approached the hotspot traditionally associated with "Angry Dan."

The locals reported to us many paranormal anomalies as well as apparition sightings – all events that continue to occur into the present throughout this paranormally active town.

For newbie ghost hunters (we *do* have years of experience as trained field investigators for the Mutual UFO Network), we thought this was a successful investigation, introducing ourselves to the equipment and testing our mettle against spirit anomalies.

Did we make mistakes? Most definitely.

- Kym forgot to hit the start button on her spirit box at one point, marveling at the total absence of spirit communication.

- Mark took breathtaking pictures of the contextual landscape but had inadvertently flipped the settings of his SLR camera to manual, overexposing all his photographs.
- Mark also left on the beeper of his EMF meter during an audio-only recording session, making it impossible to hear anything during later analysis.
- He also had a tendency to continue talking during audio-only recordings, not allowing any spirits who wanted to communicate a chance to respond.
- Kym failed to plug in her tablet the night before and had to wait for a recharge before she could participate in some portions of the investigation.
- Our team, after carting around the camcorder to various rooms in the courthouse, got tired of the hassle and failed to document one of our best pieces of evidence.

But we got our feet wet.

If there's a lesson to be learned here, it's to get familiar with your equipment before arriving at the haunted hotels described in the rest of this book.

WILD WEST GHOSTS

Chapter One
Creede

Creede Hotel & Restaurant B&B

The Creede Hotel & Restaurant B&B

120 N. Main, Creede, CO 81130
(719) 658-2608
creedehotel.com

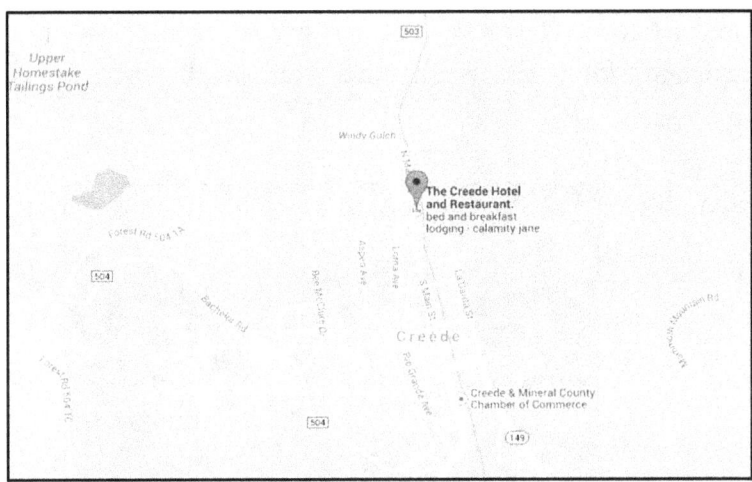

Google Map

Season: May through September
Peak: July and August (reservations encouraged in advance)
Pet friendly: No
Family friendly: Yes
WiFi: Yes

Description, Ambience, Furnishings

The ambience of The Creede Hotel starts at the city limits. The town preserves much of the architecture of its Wild West beginnings; the people are friendly and nearly every pickup carts two or three large, shaggy dogs in its bed.

The hotel, situated on the north end of Main Street next to the popular Creede Repertory Theater, is easy to spot with its white clapboard siding and bright blue trim on all posts, doors, and windows.

The Restaurant

Three Main Street doors lead to the interior – one to the restaurant and front desk, one to the Western Room, and one directly to the stairs leading to the guestrooms.

Bannister rails surround the second-floor balcony complemented by white lattice trim on the covered overhang of the sidewalk beneath. A wrought-iron and wooden-plank bench rests by the front door for anyone who wants to watch the town go by.

Downtown Creede from second-story balcony

Hardwood floors and rustic wooden wainscoting decorate the restaurant/bar, where six days a week guests and the public can enjoy a casual lunch and upscale dinner such as bleu cheese-encrusted filet mignon and fresh fish flown in overnight from Honolulu. The restaurant offers breakfast for hotels guests every day. The journal entries in the guestrooms testify to the excellence of the cuisine and the hospitality of the staff.

A full-service bar extends across one end of the dining room, adjoined by a unique registration desk constructed of the wood from a dismantled antique piano. The walls display work by well-known watercolorist Steve Quiller (who also owns a gallery down the block). The attached Western Room offers additional seating as does the open patio. Suitable for conferences, weddings, and special events, the entire facility can accommodate groups of up to two-hundred. Signed movie posters and other western décor cover the walls of the Western Room.

Each of the four upstairs guestrooms bears the name of an infamous previous boarder: Poker Alice, Calamity Jane, Bat Masterson, and Soapy Smith. Three rooms contain connecting private baths, and one a personal bath at the end of the hall. Two rooms open to the outside covered balcony, and each features one antique double bed with the charming furnishings and look of yesteryear.

According to hotel owner/chef David Toole, he's tried to keep the feel of the Old West. We think he's succeeded.

PAST AND PRESENT

Hopeful prospectors worked the canyons surrounding Creede after the first silver strike in 1869, but the region remained too remote to make mining profitable for years. Ranching and homesteading followed when stage stations reached the area by the 1870s, but the three tiny communities of Stringtown, Jimtown, and Amethyst remained small and struggling until a miner named Nicholas Creede discovered a rich vein of silver in nearby East Willow Creek Canyon in 1889.

Legend has it Creede declared, "Holy Moses, I've struck it rich!" and his Holy Moses Mine launched Colorado's last great silver boomtown. Over the next two years, the communities swelled from 600 locals to well over 10,000, spilling over six miles and consuming the other settlements under the name of Creede. Soon the Denver & Rio Grande Railroad began serving the area's mines. Life was good.

The boomtown days were wild times, drawing notorious figures such as gambler Robert Ford, who'd killed Jesse James. A disgruntled gamer named O'Kelley later shot Ford in the back inside his tent-saloon, but he was pardoned for ridding the town of Ford's monopoly on gambling. Still, organized graft soon fell to the wiles of Soapy Smith, who operated an extortion racket from the Orleans Club, taking a cut from saloons, brothels, and gaming houses throughout the town.

Other infamous individuals drawn to Creede included Bat Masterson and William Sidney "Cap" Light (the town's first deputy sheriff, also the brother-in-law of Soapy Smith).

Creede boasted a hundred lodging establishments at the time, and the Creede Hotel, then Zang's Hotel (after its owner), was hailed as one of the town's finest. John Zang, a Denver brewer, had come to Creede to distribute his beer, building the hotel along with a saloon and brothel.

In the 1890s the hotel included rooms, saloon, and brothel.

No structure in Creede was ever grand or elaborate – buildings were thrown up as quickly as possible – and Zang's Hotel was no exception. Still, the hotel was the fanciest place in town to stay, and Smith, Ford, Poker Alice Tubbs, and Calamity Jane all boarded there at one time or another.

Poker Alice worked gambling rooms throughout mining towns in Colorado, usually puffing on a black stogie. She became a well-known figure at Bob Ford's Creede Exchange. She once remarked, "I'd rather play poker with five or six experts than eat."

Known for her wild tales, Calamity Jane (Martha Jane Canary) also played cards like a pro, wore only men's clothing, and had the reputation of out-drinking any man at the bar. She lived in Creede for a time, playing poker at local saloons.

Fires ravaged Creede twice around the turn of the century, both times sparing Zang's Hotel.

When silver prices fell in 1893, Soapy Smith headed north to the Klondike. With anti-gaming reforms lifted in Denver the previous year, many others drifted away from town also following the silver price panic. Creede's boom days were over.

After operating the hotel for a number of years, Zang met with an unfortunate end. In June of 1911, Zang broke into a home, made unwanted advances, and attacked a woman who shot and killed him. Mrs. Zang retained and operated the hotel until 1919.

The town survived on lead and zinc in the local ores through much of the Twentieth Century, but the last railroad run ended by 1973. These days, the town continues as a tourist and outdoor recreation center.

The Creede Hotel remains the town's oldest lodging and dining establishment, and visitors can overnight in restored guestrooms that once served as home to many of Creede's colorful and notorious characters.

The current owner, David Toole, has operated the business since 2000, and he lives in the building's quarters that once served as the brothel. The bar still attracts celebrities, including politicians and at one point western icon John Wayne who owned property near the town.

LEGENDS, STORIES, AND GUEST EXPERIENCES

Most who've worked at The Creede Hotel have a ghost story to tell. Leslie Heller, hotel manager for a decade, has found the pictures running the length of hall next to the bar askew every morning. She's also felt an invisible presence on a regular basis. A few days before we interviewed her, she heard a whistled tune coming from the bar, which was empty. She didn't recognize the song, and when she whistled it for us, we didn't either.

She often sees movement out of the corner of her eye in the morning before other staffers arrive. That may well be: The former manager saw an apparition of a woman at the front desk in the restaurant and carried on a brief conversation before the figure disappeared before his eyes.

One evening, a restaurant waitperson headed toward the kitchen with trays full of dishes, wondering how she would manage the door. She needn't have worried. An unseen hand opened the door for her and closed it politely behind.

During the summer of 2014, an intern staffer from Europe captured with a camera the image of a Victorian-dressed woman in the antique mirror in the Western Room. The photo revealed a figure with a rather long neck twisted awkwardly to the side in a pose resembling someone dangling from a hangman's noose.

A staff member captured on camera a mysterious woman figure in this mirror.

Sometimes, upstairs guests experience their own share of ghostly encounters. Each guestroom contains a journal to record impressions of their stay. One entry in the Poker Alice Room states, "Besides the ghost presence on our last night ... the glasses on the nightstand were falling off one by one. When I picked them up this morning, there were seven on the floor."

Other guests have reported footsteps walking up and down the stairwell.

Although David seldom encounters ghostly activity himself, he said he occasionally senses unseen presences: "I feel like they appreciate me taking care of the place and leave me alone."

Our Personal Experiences

Since we visited before the hotel opened for its summer season, David and Leslie left the premises and gave us the run of the place to conduct our investigation. This arrangement worked for us because that eliminated external noise and the possibility of contaminated EVPs. (Recall from the introduction that EVP stands for **E**lectronic **V**oice **P**henomenon, either through a digital recorder or a spirit box.)

They recommended the Calamity Jane Room and the Poker Alice Room – the two guestrooms with the most reported paranormal activity. We headed up the narrow staircase and started with an EMF sweep of these two rooms and the hallway. (Again, recall from the introduction that EMF stands for **E**lectro**m**agnetic **F**ield, and EM field strengths may indicate ghosts are present or trying to communicate.) At the mouth of the stairwell, the meter showed 380mG and climbed to a steady 460mG near the bathroom at the other end of the hall. The EM field in the Calamity Jane Room registered 400mG on the east side, 530 over the bed, and mid 600s by the balcony. These readings were our baseline measurements to compare against any anomalies.

We set up our camcorder, digital recorder, flashlight, and spirit box to start our first session. We introduced ourselves, explained our equipment to any invisible presences, and invited them to speak with us or manipulate the flashlight. The light remained steady throughout the time in this room, and we'd have

Many paranormal events occur in the Calamity Jane Room.

Calamity Jane

to wait until we returned home to analyze the digital audio recordings. We observed EMF fluctuations from 530mG to 570mG while we asked for interaction.

However, the spirit box managed to produce a number of EVPs we could hear at the time. We asked if any spirits were here to talk to us and heard a quick response of "Here?" We weren't alone in the hotel after all. So we asked again how many spirits shared the room with us and twice we heard, "Eight" – standing room only. Then we queried their names. The first reply was "Myrtle." (We would later research that name for the vicinity and found several possibilities. Myrtle was common during the era, and a number of them lived and died in Creede.) We also heard the names "Liz" and "Fes" as well as a man's voice saying, "Death."

During our later analysis, we discovered we'd captured a woman's voice declaring, "I think I'm going to shoot you." That unexpected announcement followed a less intelligible statement by a man, and we think we recorded an exchange between the two of them rather than a threat aimed at us.

During the real-time session, Kym heard a voice coming from just beyond the open room door, so we checked the hallway expecting to see Leslie. No one in the hallway – at least, no one we could see since we were locked down and alone on the premises. But when we asked who was in the hall, a woman's voice told us, "Bob." Bob Ford? He'd died in 1892, assassinated in his nearby tent-saloon while he boarded at this establishment.

We struck camp and moved across the hall to the Poker Alice Room. On the way we noticed the slight odor of smoke – but only for a moment (a whiff of Alice's famous stogie?) Since the building displayed a no-smoking sign, we mentioned this to David in a later follow-up interview. He told us that end of the hotel was closest to the buildings that burned when fires swept through early-day Creede. Make of that what you will.

In the Poker Alice Room, we followed the same routine for the next session. We recorded 500mG throughout the room and 550mG over the bed (metal bedsprings may have elevated these stable readings.)

Again, no interaction with the flashlight. But the spirit box captured multiple names and phrases. Most intriguing was "Alice" – given the room bore her name and we know she boarded in this facility. We also recorded the name "David" and the word "Brave." Other phrases proved more perplexing, including some clear and some garbled words but each delivered by separate voices. One asked the question, "You have the two (boys?)?" Another proclaimed, "Bless you," and still another said, "Come to (me?)."

We decided to run an experiment on the dresser where a spirit had knocked over seven consecutive glasses. We set up two coffee mugs near the edge and invited the spirit to repeat the event. After ten minutes, the mugs remained in place. In later analysis, we discovered on the digital audio recording a response to our question, "Did you knock the glasses over?" (in front of the former guest). The immediate answer was a whispered "Yes."

The nightstand/dresser in the Poker Alice Room, also very haunted

That was all we needed to crown our investigation. Audio-only EVPs are some of the most convincing types of evidence ghost hunters capture.

Highlights of the Area

Some of the most pristine areas in the state greet visitors who want to take advantage of outdoor recreation. But the locale is steeped in Old West and mining history, represented by such colorful characters as Calamity Jane, Poker Alice and Bob Ford. Preserved architecture and friendly people fill this charming frontier town situated just a few miles from the headwaters of the Rio Grande River.

Creede Chamber of Commerce
904 S. Main St., Creede, CO 81130
(719) 658-2374
creede.com

Annual Festivals
- Taste of Creede Festival – May
- Small Print Show – May/June
- Creede Chute Out Rodeo – July
- July 4th Festival – July
- Woodcarvers Rendezvous – July
- Creede Rock & Mineral Show – August
- Headwaters New Play Festival – August
- Cruisin' the Canyon Car Show – September
- Labor Day Weekend Celebration – September
  ATV Rodeo
  Balloon Festival
  Gravity Derby
  Mountain Run
- Chocolate Festival – November

Cultural/Recreational Opportunities
- Creede Historical Museum
  Historical artifacts and walking tours
  Creede, CO
  (719) 658-2004
  creedehistoricalsociety.com

- Creede Repertory Theatre
  Nationally acclaimed theater entertainment
  Main Street, Creede, CO

(866) 658-2540
creederep.org

- Creede Underground Mining Museum
  Mining displays
  503 Forest Service Rd. #9, Creede, CO
  (719) 658-0811
  undergroundminingmuseum.com

- Rio Grande National Forest
  Almost two million acres of national forest
  Creede, CO
  (719) 852-5941
  fs.usda.gov/riogrande

- Silver Thread Byway
  Scenic drive from Creede to Lake City, CO
  Colorado Hwy. 149, Creede, CO
  sangres.com/colorado/scenic-byways/silverthread1.htm

More
- Central Colorado/Creede
  centralcolorado.com/creede.htm

- Mountain Views/Creed
  mountainviewsrv.com/all-events-festivals/creede-events-festivals.html

WILD WEST GHOSTS

Chapter Two
Crested Butte

Forest Queen Hotel

FOREST QUEEN HOTEL

129 Elk Ave, Crested Butte, CO 81224
(970) 349-0236
forestqueenhotel.com

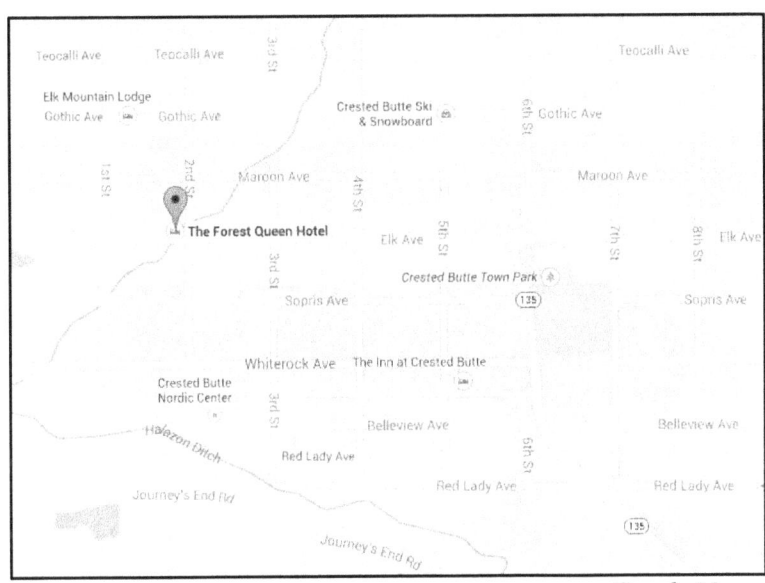

Google Map

Season: Year round
Peak: Winter and summer
Pet friendly: No
Family friendly: Yes
WiFi: Yes

DESCRIPTION, AMBIENCE, FURNISHINGS

The Forest Queen is housed on the second floor of a wood-framed and clapboard-sided building with violet- and red-trimmed windows and doors. Like many establishments in the Old West, the structure boasts the typical two-and-a-half-story façade supported by ornate exterior pillars. An outdoor patio allows guests to enjoy people-watching, mountain scenery, and Coal Creek, which runs alongside the hotel and through the town. Because of Crested Butte's building code to retain the flavor of the frontier, additional restored shops along Elk Avenue contribute to the ambience.

Coal Creek Grill

Coal Creek Grill shares the building, the entire layout of the two separate businesses resembling the architecture of an1800s ground-floor saloon and upstairs brothel. In fact, restaurant patrons – just like saloon patrons – can step from the bar to the stairwell without having to go outside. These days an additional exterior door also opens to the steep flight of narrow stairs leading to the guestrooms. It's not hard to imagine dancehall doves escorting their clients up the steps to their special rooms.

We liked the feel of *stepping* back in time and experiencing a by-gone era when we walked down the antiquated hallway. Seven Victorian-styled rooms offer a choice of private or shared baths in varying configurations of queen, double, or twin beds. Each features at least one brass bed and period furniture.

Because Crested Butte is a ski town, guests who stay at the Forest Queen have the opportunity to sample many fine eateries in the community, including a number of five-star restaurants. We chose the attached Coal Creek Grill – open, sunny, and an overall pleasant atmosphere furnished with tables and chairs as well as a full bar. We recommend the "New Mexico Philly" with portions too large to eat in a single sitting.

Past and Present

The vicinity of Crested Butte in the East River Valley served as the summer home to the nomadic Ute Indians for hundreds of years. By the Nineteenth Century, they shared the land with trappers, explorers, and early attempts at settlement.

Eager miners followed earlier pioneers when prospectors discovered silver in the late 1860s. Within ten years, coal and silver mines opened in the surrounding area, resulting in multiple smaller mining towns. Widespread timber harvesting supplied lumber and fuel for newcomers while emerging cattle operations helped contribute to the economy by the 1870s. Crested Butte became the principal supply center and an official town in 1880. The Denver Rio Grande Railroad arrived the year after.

Mining proved dangerous work. On Jan. 24, 1884, a coal mine shaft ignited and exploded, launching coal cars out of the tunnel, scattering debris more than a hundred feet, and destroying nearby buildings. A rescue attempt recovered fifty-nine bodies, many of them teenaged boys.

The Forest Queen Hotel began operating in the early days as part of Crested Butte's red-light district, a series of brothels lined up between First Street and Second Street on Elk Avenue. The original building consisted of a saloon filling the first floor and a brothel on the second.

After the mining decline of 1893, Crested Butte survived, in part, because of the high-grade coal mines, some of which continued operations into the early 1950s. Higher transportation costs and lower consumption of coal eventually forced most of the mines to close, along with the railroad.

In 1961 scouts came to Crested Butte to investigate the area for a possible ski mountain. After a decade of slow times, locals welcomed the new opportunity.

In keeping with a newer era, the Forest Queen had transformed into a more respectable business, with a series of taverns and restaurants occupying the first floor while the second floor provided accommodations to overnight guests and longer-term boarders.

Today, Crested Butte not only hosts a thriving ski industry but also boasts a recreational playground for biking, hiking, and other outdoor pastimes. Shops, restaurants, and a slate of cultural events and festivities draw thousands of visitors year round to this community of 1,500 full-time residents.

LEGENDS, STORIES, AND GUEST EXPERIENCES

Guests and staff have reported paranormal goings-on at both the hotel and grill for many years. Housekeeping staff say they find rearranged or tousled bed sheets and linens in the rooms on a regular basis. One chef from the kitchen below stayed upstairs overnight in a room with two beds. Awaking the next morning, he found the clothes he'd left in his suitcase removed and arranged on the other bed – not a service the hotel provides.

Another chef told us accounts of items that regularly turn up missing in the kitchen, only to return a day or two later. These are industrial utensils, nothing an individual would borrow for home use.

Perhaps the most famous haunting in the hotel involves an 1800s prostitute named "Elizabeth." Many locals refer to her as the Red Lady Ghost. Her tragic tale circulates in two versions, both ending with hurling herself from a second-story window, headfirst to her death in Coal Creek. The first version relates that one of Elizabeth's regulars, a patron she adored, promised to deliver her from a sordid life. But one day she looked out her window and saw him kissing his wife – and thus the suicide.

Coal Creek, where Elizabeth allegedly plunged to her death.

The other version tells the story this way: While Elizabeth stayed at the hotel, she fell in love with an itinerant gambler who talked her into bankrolling her life's savings. She did so to win his affection. But after the gambler doubled his winnings, he abandoned her with no money and no prospects – again ending with the leap from her window.

Guests and staffers alike report the Red Lady Ghost makes her presence known by banging pots and pans and slamming doors. Her alleged crib is present-day Room Four.

Both the men's and women's bathrooms in the grill also have a history of paranormal activity. One patron had a cellphone knocked from his hand before he turned on the light switch. When he bent to retrieve the cell, something prevented him from straightening back up for several seconds. Once upright, he turned on the light to an empty room. On a different occasion, a woman experienced a series of repeated lights-out episodes in the women's bathroom down that same hallway.

The reports of paranormal activity don't stop in this building. In the next block, the Eldo Brew Pub has a reputation for hauntings as well, with staff reporting apparitions and anomalous sounds of all sorts. Indeed, most of the buildings on Elk Avenue hold ghostly tales. Talk to any local.

Our Personal Experiences

We began by interviewing the staff in the restaurant below the hotel. They had lots to say (which we included in the above section) and recommended we start our investigations in Rooms One, Four, and Six.

We had the unusual advantage of arriving on a day when the hotel was unoccupied, and the manager gave us a master key to the entire second floor of guest rooms. She left us to our own devices, literally.

Opening the rooms, we peered inside each and took baseline readings, which ranged from 200-460mG. In the hallway, we noted the smell of old smoke, like the aftermath of charred timbers. Later we asked one of the restaurant staff about it, and she said she and the cook had noticed the same odd odor for the first time that very morning.

The second-floor hallway of the former brothel-turned-hotel.

From the hallway, we entered Room Six and stopped in our tracks, asking each other if the room felt weird. The space raised the hair on both of our necks. We returned to Room One to organize our equipment. In the meantime, we decided to let the video camera roll inside Room Six. Before we opened our videocam case in the creepy room, we discovered one of the bed pillows now on the floor. We exchanged glances and sang the Twilight Zone tune.

Back in Room One, we started an EVP session, followed by EMF and spirit box readings. The EMF meter registered 300-500mG while we worked, once spiking to 700mG near the foot of the brass bed (and nowhere else over the rest of the brass). At the same time, the spirit box chattered away, including such intriguing words as "Burning" (twice), "Death," and "Explosive." We experienced similar phenomena in Room Four: the spirit box announcing "Game," "Innocence," and "Gate" (twice), but no significant EMF spikes. We'd expected more activity since poor

Elizabeth had thrown herself out of that bedroom window.

(More on this later, after we analyzed our findings back home.)

With some trepidation, we reentered Room Six – and here we hit the mother lode. Both our EMF meters went off the charts, Mark's sounding high-pitched beeps and Kym's emitting a siren alert and once flashing an odd orb on the meter display we'd never seen before. Most of the room revealed hotspots, particularly on and around the bed. We conducted an EVP session, asking for a sign of any spirit's presence. At that moment, one of the table lamps flickered once (the only flicker to take place that day). Afterward, Kym turned on her spirit box, which produced the words "Horse," "Rifle," "Room," ""Burning," and "Fire."

Kym returned to Room One to retrieve the rest of our equipment and found the door shut and locked. We'd left it wide open. (To be fair, the window was open, but no breeze or draft blew through the second floor that day.) In the meantime, Mark started his spirit box in Room Six, which seemed strangely quiet. It said only two words: "Secret" and "Kym."

Room Six, where our spirit box said Kym's name

Needless to say, Kym felt a little disturbed by the direct reference. More so, since she confessed she'd felt the sensation of dragging hobble ropes or shackles around her ankles as soon as we'd entered the second floor: Each step would pull at the right ankle while the left one felt a pinch. The feeling persisted most of the time we remained in the hotel but stopped as soon as we left the building. Let's get this straight – Kym has always been the "Scully" of the investigations, pragmatic, rational, skeptical.

About that time, we both heard loud footfalls in the hallway and a door slam – a form of paranormal activity often reported on the second floor. We peered out, expecting to see the manager, but we were alone. All the doors remained open.

Our later analyses detected no orbs in the photos, no anomalies in video footage. However, we did identify one EVP of a woman's voice in Room Four, but neither of us could make out what her three syllables actually said. Recall this is the room where poor Elizabeth had plunged out the window to her death in the creek running right beside the hotel. We couldn't help but wonder if we'd captured Elizabeth's voice with our audio-only recording.

This was the room (#4) occupied by Elizabeth.

One more thing to report: When we got home, Kym found a red straight-line pinch bruise on the inside of her left ankle where she'd felt the "shackles" sensation, and which we photographed before it faded within a couple of hours.

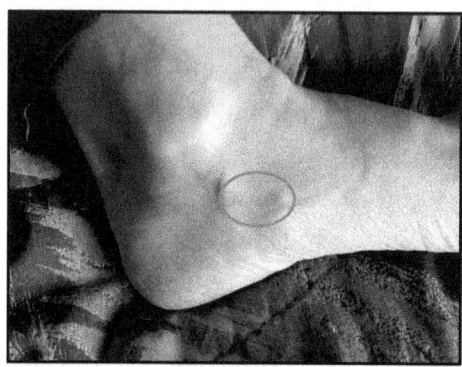

The bruise Kym sustained from a ghostly pinch

Highlights of the Area

Known as "the last great ski town," Crested Butte offers a rare mix of history and adventure all year round. Epic trails and scenery cater to visitors who yearn for pristine beauty; a myriad of festivals and events combine family fun along with world-class entertainers. Experience the town's one-of-a-kind shops, unique galleries, and 5-star restaurants.

Crested Butte/Mt. Crested Butte Chamber of Commerce
601 Elk Ave., Crested Butte, CO 81224
(970) 349-6438
cbchamber.com

Gunnison Chamber of Commerce
500 E. Tomichi Ave., Gunnison, CO 81230

(970) 641-1501
gunnison-co.com

Annual Festivals
- Flauschink Spring Festival – First week of April
- Crested Butte Bike Week – June
- Crested Butte Music Festival Series – June to August
- Crested Butte Wildflower Festival – July
- Crested Butte Wine & Food Festival – July
- Independence Day Celebration – July
- Crested Butte Festival of the Arts – July/August
- Crested Butte Chili & Beer Festival – September
- Crested Butte Film Festival Series – September
- Vinotok Fall Harvest Festival – September

Cultural/Recreational Opportunities
- Black Canyon of the Gunnison
  Some of the steepest cliffs and oldest rock in the U.S.
  Gunnison, CO
  (970) 641-2337
  nps.gov/blca

- Club at Crested Butte
  High-country golfing
  385 Country Club Dr., Crested Butte, CO
  (970) 349-6127
  theclubatcrestedbutte.com

- Crested Butte Center for the Arts
  Performing arts
  403 2nd St., Crested Butte, CO
  (970) 349-0366
  cbmountaintheatre.org

- Crested Butte Heritage Museum
  Historical memorabilia
  331 Elk Ave., Crested Butte, CO
  (970) 349-1880
  crestedbuttemuseum.com

- Crested Butte Mountain Resort
  Alpine skiing
  500 Gothic Rd., Mt. Crested Butte, CO
  (970) 349-2222
  skicb.com

- Trailhead Children's Museum
  Hands-on fun for kids
  19 Emmons Rd., Crested Butte, CO
  (970) 349-7160
  trailheadkids.org

More

- Gunnison/Crested Butte Tourism
  gunnisoncrestedbutte.com

- Colorado Info
  coloradoinfo.com/summervacationplanner/gunnison-crestedbutte

Chapter Three
Cripple Creek

Hotel St. Nicholas

Hotel St. Nicholas

303 3rd St, Cripple Creek, CO 80813
(719) 689-0856
HotelStNicholas.com

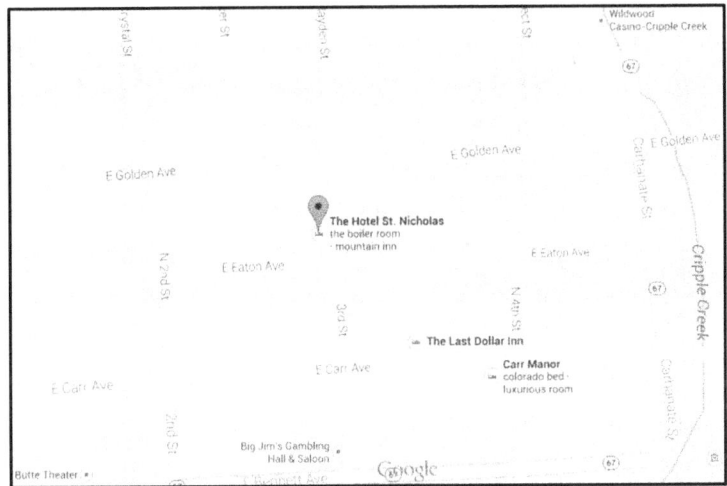

Google Map

Season: Year round
Peak: June through September
Pet friendly: No
Family friendly: Yes
WiFi: Yes

DESCRIPTION, AMBIENCE, FURNISHINGS

Shades of Alfred Hitchcock – but with a lot more class. Because this building is a renovation of a former Sisters of Mercy hospital and sits elevated on a hill above the town, the setting resembles the classic haunted hotel. The three-story brick building, shrouded by tall Ponderosa pines, appears imposing and impressive with outside balconies and a cupola still topped with an iconic Christian cross.

If the outside doesn't make you catch your breath, the inside will – whether you're a ghost hunter or not.

Upon entering the lobby, you'll first notice a unique enclosed mauve-painted cashier booth trimmed in gold and green. Period furniture and surrounding wallpaper are reminiscent of turn-of-the-century décor. A pleasant dining room for continental breakfasts flanks one side of the lobby, and a cozy full-service lounge sits on the other side. Down the hall, a special events room, complete with pool table and fireplace, accommodates parties of up to forty-five people.

Guests can enjoy a continental breakfast.

A roof-top Jacuzzi offers views of not only the downtown but also the breathtaking Sangre de Cristo Mountains. Around the corner from the Jacuzzi is a dry sauna.

Stamped-tin ceilings on the first level, hardwood flooring with oriental rugs, and rich original woodwork throughout – all these features accent wide hallways and a central staircase connecting the three floors.

Each of the hotel's fifteen rooms is uniquely themed, variously containing queen, double, and single beds. All include a private bath and cable TV. However, the facility ingeniously retains the architecture of the original hospital. The ward room, which once served multiple patients, now features a spacious accommodation with full bathroom and separate shower. The former nuns' quarters now configures a suite with sitting room, TV room, hallway, and bedroom. And the old surgery-turned-guestroom still opens with double gurney doors at the top of a small ramp.

More modern amenities include free WiFi, fax, copier, and a town shuttle to gaming and local area attractions.

Past and Present

The Hotel St. Nicholas's colorful history began in 1898 when the Dublin-based Catholic Sisters of Mercy built it to accommodate the Cripple Creek area during the Colorado gold rush.

According to history compiled by the hotel, "The Sisters originally operated from an existing wood-framed building, one block from the current St. Nicholas, and served 307 patients during their first year. A massive fire in April 1896, destroyed most of Cripple Creek, and led to an incident of drama and irony.

As the fire progressed through [town], many wooden-framed buildings were dynamited in an effort to slow the fire. While the Sisters were evacuating patients to safer locations, a member of an anti-Catholic society entered the hospital's kitchen and attempted to destroy the building by placing dynamite in the stove chimney. To the man's misfortune, the dynamite exploded prematurely, causing little damage to the hospital, but blowing off his leg. He was evacuated with the other patients, and the compassionate care he received from the Sisters led him to express remorse for his deed. His shoe, which had landed in the tea kettle, was kept by the Sisters as a memento."

The nuns, convinced they needed a safer structure, hired a Denver architect to design and build a three-story brick hospital for a cost of $12,000. The first two floors served patients, reserving the third floor for the nuns and the attic for the hospital orderly. Completely modern for its day, the hospital contained electric lights, steam heat, hot and cold running water, and surgery facilities. The first patient was a young miner who had fallen down a mine shaft.

The nuns quarters while the building served as a hospital operated by the Sisters of Mercy.

The Sisters left Cripple Creek in 1924, and local doctors bought the facility. After closing in 1972, the building served as a boarding house but eventually stood vacant by the time it was purchased and refurbished as a hotel in the mid-1990s.

The current owner and proprietor is Susan Adelbush.

LEGENDS, STORIES, AND GUEST EXPERIENCES

The community abounds with ghost stories, and the Hotel St. Nicholas has its fair share. Paranormal activity occurs on all three floors.

A number of years ago, owner Susan sat working in the office behind the cashier's booth and heard someone behind her. She turned to see a tall, thin man who wore a turn-of-the-century bowler hat and long coat. Within seconds, he disappeared.

Hotel owner Susan Adelbush saw the apparition of the "bowler hat man" just inside the cashier cage.

An employee later saw that same man, wearing the same clothes, as he strolled past her out of the nuns' room and simply vanished before her eyes. Only sometime afterward did Susan and the employee compare notes to discover they had witnessed the same apparition.

Not to be ignored, the bowler-hatted gentleman appeared again to part-time local Tom Tunnicliff in the first-floor hotel lounge. He and several friends stood at the bar. The front doorbell sounded and the on-duty staffer left to check but soon returned – no one had entered the otherwise empty hotel. Tom felt someone touch his shoulder, and he turned to see the dark outlined silhouette of a man in a long coat and bowler. The apparition passed through Tom's arm, giving him a tingle, and proceeded to walk through the bar as well as through the antique boiler against the outside wall.

Guests have reported a crying little girl at the foot of their bed in Room Eleven (the former surgery room). Others said they've heard children playing with a bouncing ball and laughing on the third-floor hallway in the middle of the night. This happens even on evenings when no children stay at the hotel, according to Susan.

An article in the *Pikes Peak Courier* records that the hotel also remains home to ghostly former patients of the hospital's mental ward. The article cites another reported recurring presence – a ghost called "Stinky," sighted on the back staircase and making his presence known with a "sewage-like smell."

Hauntings occur throughout Cripple Creek. Many casinos claim to have regular ghosts that play slots. One establishment reports a recurring apparition who sits at a particular machine. The ghost plays for a while and then disappears. One wonders who collects the earnings, if any.

Several people visiting Tom Tunnicliff's own home, below the Hotel St. Nicholas, have witnessed an apparition arrive on his porch, come through a locked door, and walk through the house.

"People in Cripple Creek often dress up in period clothes," Tom said. "But sometimes they disappear. You don't know if you've seen a real person or a ghost."

OUR PERSONAL EXPERIENCES

Owner Susan gave us a walking tour of this large sprawling hotel – all three floors – pointing out along the way where various paranormal activity had taken place, including the lounge on the first floor where the apparition had walked through the wooden bar. (See above section.)

We focused, however, on the guestrooms and upstairs hallways. We started in Room One, the old nuns' quarters (when the building was a hospital), where the apparition with a derby hat and duster had appeared. The suite consisted of a sitting room with a futon bed and connecting alcove and bedroom. Our EMF baselines hovered in the low 300mG range for the alcove and bedroom, but higher in the sitting room – around 500mG. We decided to record a spirit box session in the sitting room. We heard very little in real time and in later analysis. Perhaps the man in the duster had intimidated the rest of his ghostly cohort, and he himself wasn't talking.

We were itching to get to Room Eleven, the old operating room, so we packed up and headed to the other end of the floor, up the short ramp to the room, and through the double doors – still in place from an era when hospital personnel pushed gurneys into surgery. Initial EMF readings of 300-400mG leaped to 920mG when we began our spirit box queries. From there forward, the EMF remained in the 800s. No wonder – the cacophony of voices that erupted from the box made it nearly impossible to carry on a coherent conversation at first. The spirit box chatter became so disruptive we had to ask *them* to slow down and not all speak at once. The voices did slow down a little bit, and we could pick out "Hurt," "Broken," and "Sick." When we asked one voice why he was there, the response came back "Accident." We also heard a puzzling woman's voice say, "They killed it."

Our EVPs in the former surgery room described trauma. Note the double doors for gurneys.

We encountered that phrase again in later analysis, along with a lot more we hadn't detected in real time. At one point, we felt like spectators to murmured exchanges between one male and two female voices that seemed to be involved in a medical procedure – "First up," "Godfrey" (twice), "Excuse me," and "Danke" (German for "Thank you") all came in rapid succession. In fact, we heard a lot of German inflections. We asked for names and got "Shultz" and "Ander," among others. We also heard "Anne," "Stephen," and "David," followed by a woman's voice saying "Dave hurts." The word "Fear" came up three times, as well as "Axe," "Hit," "Lung," and the phrase "I watched it." When we asked who else occupied the room, a woman's voice offered, "Kym," suggesting awareness of our own presence.

Even in real time during the on-site session, we began to feel auditory overload using the spirit box, so we trotted over to Room Six. This had once served as a ward room. The initial utterance we heard from the box was a child's voice, sounding like a play shout – the first time a child had spoken through our spirit box. Other voices soon drowned out that first one and, no matter how many times we asked the child to talk again, we never heard it. In later analysis, we isolated a number of clear utterances in response to our queries. We had asked if someone could turn off the flashlight, getting an immediate "no" in a man's voice. When Kym asked why not, a woman responded, "Weak." We asked for names and received "Opfer" (German for "Victim") and "Bob" twice. In response to our question of what happened in that room, different spirit box voices said, "Fear" and "Help me." We asked what scared them and a woman's voice responded, "Murphy." Right before we left the room, a man with a German accent said, "Good luck."

Here's where we heard a child's EVP voice.

Our final stop was up the stairs to the third-floor hallway. This area had received comments about children playing outside guestrooms. The EMF readings in the hall were in the 590mG range with little fluctuation during that session. We once again asked for someone to turn off the flashlight and a voice responded, "No." We asked who was there and got "Me," soon followed by "Bob" and "Fred." We again detected German inflections and asked in that language if any of the spirits were from Germany. The reply was "Ja." Later analysis confirmed "Ja" again, and followed by "Deutsch."

Where German seemed to be the preferred language on our spirit box.

During our time at the hotel, we never encountered the apparition in tall hat and duster. Maybe the German spirit? We hope some of the amateur ghost hunters using this guide have the "good luck" to see him themselves.

Linda Goodman's Miracle Inn/Last Dollar Inn B&B

Linda Goodman's Miracle Inn/Last Dollar Inn B&B

315 E Carr Ave, Cripple Creek, CO 80813
(719) 689-9113
lastdollarinn.com

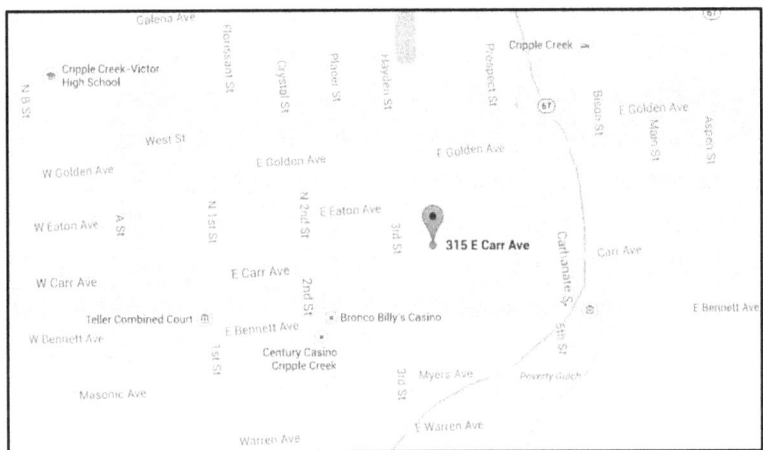

Google Map

Season: Year round
Peak: June through October (and special events in Cripple Creek)
Pet friendly: Not suitable
Family friendly: Not suitable for children under 16
WiFi: Yes

Description, Ambience, Furnishings

Linda Goodman's Miracle Inn/Last Dollar Inn B&B consists of an 1890s brownstone connected to a reconstructed Victorian-style house – not readily apparent from the outside that both buildings comprise a single inn. At the parking area, a set of stairs leads to manicured lawn and well-kept building exteriors, with arched trellis, replica antique gaslights, and lawn furniture. In their unique ways, both structures feature bay windows.

Owners Jason Barton and Sofia Balas greeted us as we stepped inside. The décor dazzled us with its deep red color scheme, rich carpets, floral wallpaper, and delicate period furnishings. Nothing in the inn looks placed by accident: Each pillow, doll, and vase appears lovingly chosen and situated. Colored light spills into the parlor through a stained-glass depiction of an almost life-sized St. Francis holding a dove. The effect is almost museum like. North of the parlor, a dining room adjoins both a sitting alcove and a kitchen attached to a gallery (once the maid's quarters) displaying owner Sofia's paintings as well as crafts by other community artisans. All art is for sale.

Linda Goodman installed this stained-glass portrait of St. Francis while she owned the house.

Goodman and others witnessed a full-bodied apparition of Nikola Tesla in this corner of the lobby. Note the portrait of Goodman on the wall.

The B&B still honors former owner and author/astrologist Linda Goodman by displaying her portrait, her books, and the picture of one of her parents. Even her original bedroom bears her name on the door.

An open stairway leads directly to four guestrooms in the original inn –the location of reported paranormal activity. A second-floor hallway connects to the newer Victorian house, providing two rooms for guests who prefer to avoid ghosts. We spent most of our time in the older building, but the walk to the newer part was seamless in character.

Each room contains different décor, with antique bed frames and distinctive wallpaper. A personal touch adds warmth with a variety of accents such as skirted bedside tables, period wall hangings, and porcelain ornaments. All six rooms maintain the Victorian motif, three containing oversized full beds, two with queens, and one with a king. Each includes a private bath.

Both Jason and Sofia felt drawn to the inn well before they bought it. But in the end, according to Sofia, "The house chose us." We agree.

Past and Present

Cripple Creek's 1800s history began as a cattle pasture before Bob Womack discovered an ore deposit in 1890 and sparked the last great Colorado gold rush. Soon after, prospectors flooded the region, increasing the population from 500 to 10,000 people in three years.

In 1896, three successive fires destroyed most of the city. Resourceful citizens rebuilt Cripple Creek over the next few months, and many of the historic buildings still in existence date back to that renovation.

These days, only a few small mines still operate. The real gold comes from local gambling casinos, legalized in 1991, and they now occupy many of the historic buildings.

Shortly after the 1896 fires, a new city ordinance required builders to use brick. A gentleman from the East Coast moved to town and built what would later become Linda Goodman's Miracle Inn. He modeled his new home after the brownstone style he was accustomed to and erected it next door to a boarding house. In the decades that followed, the inn also became a boarding house, a bookkeeping office, and a private residence. Legend holds that ladies of the night operated out of the rooms.

The bay window in the Goodman Room overlooking Cripple Creek once served as a lookout by brothel owners after prostitution became illegal.

Even Nicola Tesla reportedly stayed there during some of his Colorado electrical experiments.

During the 1960s, author Leland Feitz summered in the house. After meeting fellow author Linda Goodman (*Sun Signs*) at a book signing, he invited her to Cripple Creek. Soon after, she rented the house and eventually bought it, adding her own touches, including the large stained glass window of St. Francis of Assisi.

Rick and Janice Woods bought the building in the 1990s. They also purchased the neighboring boarding house, reconstructing it in a Victorian style and adjoining it to the brownstone to open the Last Dollar Inn.

Jason Barton and Sofia Balas purchased the historic inn in 2013, in the eleventh hour before the building faced auction and an uncertain future. They've kept much of the décor of the original house intact, including many of Goodman's antiques and memorabilia. The B&B's guestrooms are dedicated to various former residents as well as to notorious Cripple Creek madam Pearl DeVere.

Legends, Stories, and Guest Experiences

The house has a long-time reputation for hauntings, and this feature is an attraction for many guests.

A psychic told Jason and Sofia the basement of the brownstone contains a spirit portal. If this is true, the ghosts certainly don't stay downstairs.

Even before the couple purchased the B&B, they experienced paranormal activity during a vacation stay. Opting for the Linda Goodman Room, they witnessed the door open and slam by itself (in the absence of any draft). Sofia saw a picture in the bathroom shift and move on its own. They also heard someone sitting in a wicker chair and sensed a presence standing by their bed watching them. More impressive, they observed a shadow walk past their door. In the Womack Room, Sofia witnessed a shadow apparition pass through the closed closet door.

Other guests report footsteps in the hallway, and a number have experienced their hair pulled from behind. One previous inn owner felt an unseen presence pat the top of his head while he leaned over the bed in the Linda Goodman Room. That owner also reported the door to the Feitz Room mysteriously closing and locking on its own.

According to an article in the *Pikes Peak Courier*, some guests have heard a "phantom train" while staying in the Feitz and DeVere rooms; a child ghost has appeared at the desk in one of the rooms, and the apparition of a train conductor has shown up in the living room.

Sofia has felt a cold spot move through her while serving breakfast, an activity that often happens while she sits at the table. Guests have also noted the moving cold spot in the dining room.

In the living room, Linda Goodman reported seeing the full-bodied apparition of Nikola Tesla on more than one occasion. His apparition appeared near the spot where her portrait now hangs.

Our Personal Experiences

The owners told us the inn's paranormal activity occurred in the original western building, primarily in the upstairs guestrooms and hallway. We hoped to conduct our first investigation in the Linda Goodman Room. The night before, however, that room was occupied. We still had two rooms with recent reported activity down that hallway, so we started in the Womack Room right next to Goodman's former quarters.

The EMF baseline registered 440-460mG, the same as in the adjacent hallway. We turned on a flashlight and asked spirits to create a flicker or turn it off. At that moment, the EMF jumped to 620mG, but the flashlight remained steady.

We then asked the apparition that had walked through the closet door (see previous section, Legends, Stories, and Guest Experiences) to show itself or give us a sign. No takers.

A previous investigator staying in the Womack Room experienced numerous equipment anomalies. The current owners witnessed a shadow figure pass through this closet door.

We had better luck with the spirit box, which spit out a continuous stream of words. On later EVP analysis, we discovered multiple words that related directly to the hotel: "Sofia" (our innkeeper's name) twice – once in a man's voice and once in a woman's – and then "house ... forever" in a woman's voice, and also the name "Linda." Toward the end of the session, we heard "done" three times. During the original recording, we had only heard "Leave" clearly, which we took as a dismissal.

So we packed up our gear and moved into the Leland Feitz Room, where Nikola Tesla had once stayed for three months. Our baseline EMF readings were 490-500s mG. We also had a 50 percent battery drain in our voice recorder within minutes (ironic, since it was Tesla's room!) Not uncommon in investigations where there is a strong paranormal presence. Our camcorder shut down twice – that *is* unusual.

Our spirit box was strangely quiet compared to the previous room, only giving us the words "Baseball" and "Help Feitz" (rhyming with "feats" instead of "fights," so maybe not the right name – unless his name was also sometimes pronounced the other way by folks who didn't know German pronunciation). We heard a few other utterances, including possible names, but we couldn't confirm or agree on what they said. Later EVP analysis revealed nothing more.

We flipped on the flashlight – but it wouldn't respond. Mark took it into the hall and tore it apart, checked the batteries, and reassembled. This time it worked but no spirits responded to our requests to dim or turn it off.

Nikola Tesla spent three months staying in the Feitz Room while conducting nearby electrical experiments. All our equipment batteries drained as soon as we entered this room.

Leaving the flashlight on, we returned to the Womack Room. Bam, the light turned off. Thinking we had faulty equipment,

Mark stepped back into the hall again and the flashlight worked. He stepped back into the Womack Room. Dead. Back into the hall again, on. Back in the Womack Room, dead. We decided this deserved another EVP session. We asked if spirits were messing with our equipment and got an immediate "Yeah." (We had no other malfunctions using this flashlight in our subsequent investigations.) We heard nothing else definitive from the spirit box until we returned home and analyzed the recording, where we discovered a woman's voice saying, "Flash[-something]" and later a man's voice declaring, "Enough of this."

Personally, *we* hadn't had enough of this, but we seemed to have worn out our welcome for that session. When we earlier asked the closet door apparition for a sign, maybe we got one after all through the recurring electrical anomalies.

In a follow-up visit, we did have an opportunity to check out the Linda Goodman Room, where we captured several intriguing EVPs, including a voice saying, "Let me solve that." A medium personally acquainted with Goodman later confirmed to us that the voice was indeed that of the famous astrologer.

On that second visit, Kym also experienced having her hair tugged straight up although no one was nearby during that session.

Highlights of the Area

Surrounded by the Pike National Forest, the Cripple Creek vicinity offers an abundance of outdoor recreational opportunities, including hiking, biking, boating, hunting, and rock climbing. Wildlife and birding enthusiasts can enjoy ample viewing opportunities. For indoor fun, fourteen casinos treat gamers to everything from slots to roulette to poker.

Cripple Creek Chamber of Commerce
P.O. Box 650, Cripple Creek, CO 80813
(719) 689-5877
ccvchamber.com

Annual Festivals
- Cripple Creek Ice Festival – February
- Cripple Creek Rodeo –June
- Donkey Derby Days – June
- The West Art Show – June/July
- Fourth of July Celebration – July 4
- The Clouds Car Show – September
- Mt. Pisgah Speaks Cemetery Tour – September
- Mine to Mine Challenge – October
- Gold Camp Christmas – December

Cultural/Recreational Opportunities
- Butte Theater
  Original live entertainment
  139 East Bennett Ave., Cripple Creek, CO
  (719) 689-6402
  buttetheater.com

- Cripple Creek District Museum
  Historical artifacts
  5th & Bennett Ave., PO Box 1210, Cripple Creek, CO
  (719) 689-9540
  cripplecreekmuseum.com

- Cripple Creek Railroad
  Historic passenger tours
  520 E Carr St., Cripple Creek, CO
  (719) 689-2640
  cripplecreekrailroad.com

- Florissant Fossil Beds
  Rich and diverse fossil deposits
  15807 Teller County Rd. 1, Florissant, CO
  (719) 748-3253
  nps.gov/flfo

- Mollie Kathleen Gold Mine
  Gold mine tour
  9388 Highway 67, Cripple Creek, CO
  (719) 689-2466
  goldminetours.com

- Mueller State Park
  5,000 acres for recreation
  21045 Highway 67 South, Divide, CO
  (719) 687-2366
  cpw.state.co.us/placestogo/Parks/Mueller

- Rocky Mountain Dinosaur Resource Center
  Working dinosaur museum
  201 South Fairview St., Woodland Park, CO
  (719) 686-1820
  rmdrc.com

- Victor AG & Mining Museum
  Historic and mining artifacts
  2nd & Victor Ave., Victor, CO
  (719) 651-5569
  victorcolorado.com/AgMuseum.htm

- Victor Lowell Museum
  Gold mining and journalism artifacts
  Third & Victor Ave., Victor, CO
  (719) 689-5509
  victorcolorado.com/museum.htm

More
- Visit Cripple Creek
  visitcripplecreek.com

WILD WEST GHOSTS

Chapter Four
Del Norte

Windsor Hotel

WINDSOR HOTEL

605 Grand Avenue, Del Norte, CO 81132
(719) 657-9031
WindsorHotelDelNorte.com

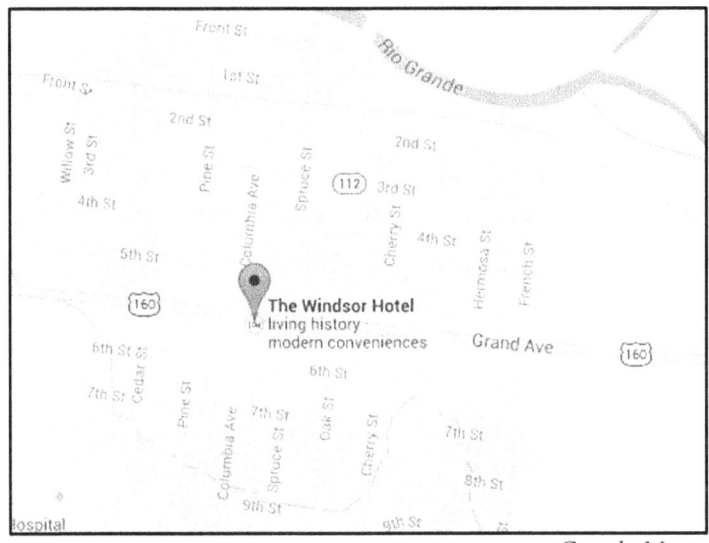

Google Map

Season: Year Round
Peak: June through mid-September
Pet friendly: No
Family friendly: Yes
WiFi: Yes

DESCRIPTION, AMBIENCE, FURNISHINGS

The Windsor Hotel stands two stories high, reminiscent of the old Spanish Territorial style of architecture – square, flat-topped, bedecked with tall narrow windows. The entire exterior has an adobe stucco finish over the brick structure.

A western motif greets visitors entering the lobby, complete with stamped-tin ceilings, heavy wooden check-in desk, antique horse-drawn carriage, and grand piano. (The hotel stages live music three nights a week.) The building maintains the original color theme throughout – muted yellow walls and pastel blue wainscoting.

The hotel features live music several nights a week in the lobby.

Lobby floors have their own story: Before renovations, a portion of the wood flooring had become damaged, but an area rancher volunteered he had a stack of the original planking in a barn. This find allowed the new owners to gather the wood and repair the damage with identical materials.

The spacious first floor includes two large event rooms for conferences, retreats, and weddings – both capable of seating thirty to fifty people. Territorial décor extends into these hospitality settings, and a multicultural courtyard flanks the building with flower planters, outside bar, and plenty of garden tables and chairs.

Beyond the front desk, a large and elegant dining room features the specialties of co-owner Regan Whitehead, a five-star chef, providing such offerings as calamari, filet of salmon, roasted trout, and other delicacies. We opted for the gilled goat cheese polenta, daily soup special, and a gourmet patty melt – all of which were superb.

The hotel accommodates conferences and private parties.

The dining room welcomes non-guests as well.

Past the dining area, a bistro bar woos clients with handcrafted cocktails, locally micro-brewed beers, and a wine list selected by certified sommelier and co-owner Kodi Whitehead.

Guests calling it a night can choose between using the original open staircase near the front door or an elevator.

If the entrance follows an Old West motif, and the hospitality rooms use Territorial design, the twenty second-floor guestrooms blend old with new. Rooms vary in configurations of king and queen beds, some suitable for couples, others for whole families.

WILD WEST GHOSTS

Guests can opt for this ornate open staircase or a nearby elevator.

Accommodations come complete with flat-screen TVs, down comforters, and hand-carved black walnut bed frames and headboards. Each room contains a private bath featuring marble shower stall and Victorian tiling. All the rooms feature air conditioning.

Remnants of bygone construction remain in exposed brick archways sectioning the hallways.

PAST AND PRESENT

The current site of the town of Del Norte falls within the vicinity of the Old Spanish Trail system used as a trade route from Santa Fe to California. By the 1870s, the area saw streams of prospectors flooding into Colorado to seek the rich deposits of gold and silver discovered in the San Juan Mountains. In 1872, the town of Del Norte sprang up on the Rio Grande River as a supplier and financial center for mining operations. At one point, freight wagons lined up on Grand Avenue for a mile waiting to head into the mining camps to the west.

In its boomtown heyday, Del Norte climbed to over 10,000 inhabitants, filled with saloons, dance halls, and local brothels as well as an opera house, movie theater, and library. During the boom years, the failure of only one vote prevented Del Norte from becoming the state capitol. In anticipation, town planners built extra wide roads capable of turning around six-horse teams.

Offsetting these high aspirations, the community experienced a Wild West town's expected share of murders, stage robberies, jail escapes, and lynchings.

According to current co-owner Steve Whitehead, the Windsor is the oldest hotel in Colorado. Enterprising citizens constructed the establishment in 1874 with local masonry and bricks. The building had expanded three times by 1888.

Note the exposed masonry marking the end of the hallway before renovation.

The hotel operated until the late 1970s, when it closed and sat empty for the next fifteen years. On the evening before scheduled demolition, Whitehead and several other locals decided to save the historic hotel. Pulling together enough funds overnight to buy the dilapidated property, they formed a committee called the Windsor Restoration and Historic Association to prevent the site's fate becoming a fast food restaurant.

From that point forward, the town joined together to preserve and later renovate the hotel. Grants and investors made it possible to restore the building above and beyond its former glory days.

Legends, Stories, and Guest Experiences

The hotel's night supervisor said she thought it unsurprising a 140-year-old hotel would be haunted – the whole town is, including the streets and other buildings. One local resident shared stories about a nearby private residence where owners had captured apparitions by accident on multiple occasions in photos of the house.

Hotel co-owner Steve Whitehead reported he witnessed a rock fly out of a door he'd just opened while conducting a tour during building renovations. No one was in that room at the time. A housekeeper said she watched undisturbed clothes hangers start to move – swinging, stopping, swinging again. The radio also suddenly came on and lights switched on and off in Room 210 while she worked.

A guest staying in Room 204 reported hearing someone vacuuming in the hallway at 1 a.m. She was about to peek out her door but the noise quit, only to begin five minutes later. Staff doesn't vacuum in the middle of the night.

Maud Heinz took her life inside this room after a failed relationship.

The most often reported site with paranormal activity is Room 209, where hotel guest Maud Heinz committed suicide in 1906. She'd arrived by train one morning, checked in under an alias, and then purchased a .38-caliber revolver and cartridges. She returned to her room and shot herself. She'd left a note, explaining her true identity, and the story soon came out. Two years earlier, she'd suffered an accident after an incident with a runaway horse, and she had "visionary spells" thereafter, according to Del Norte newspaper the *San Juan Prospector* in an article published April 7, 1906. Shortly before her death, she'd had a lover's quarrel and decided to end her life. In the century since then, guests report hearing and sometimes seeing her. Lodgers recount awakening in the middle of the night to see her peering down at them, and one awoke to hear her scream.

One of the more unusual features of the hotel lies below the south wing, accessible only from the outside courtyard: an ice cellar. The facility served double duty in the early days as a storage area to keep bodies during the winter, pending the spring thaw while remains awaited proper burial. We found no particular ghostly accounts relating to the cellar, but it certainly adds to the atmosphere!

OUR PERSONAL EXPERIENCES

Even though lodging manager Steve Whitehead told us he'd witnessed little paranormal activity himself within the hotel, our own experience in upstairs rooms began almost immediately. In fact, we got one of our favorite EVPs from an audio recording at this hotel.

We made a straight path to Room 209 – where Maud, the building's most famous ghost, resides – and followed our routine of first taking EMF readings. That room showed 500mG throughout most of the space and 580s over the bed, with surges up to 740 over the north central section of the mattress. This puzzled us since the bed consisted of black walnut frames – nothing metallic to interfere or create false readings except bedsprings.

After setting up the video camera, we started the spirit box. The real-time session produced lots of babbling, with one coherent word when we asked if the entities preferred the term spirits or ghosts. A man's voice clearly replied, "Ghosts." That word repeated itself several times throughout our investigation, possibly to make sure we got the message straight. (We made a similar query at another hotel for this book and received a similar response – at least we now have confirmations at different sites of the "PC" term to use these days!)

We brought out the flashlight and addressed Maud, asking her to use that energy to communicate. The device wouldn't turn on. We tried it again and this time the light remained steady. We left the flashlight on for several minutes before Mark picked up the unit to click it off, but without touching any buttons, the light winked and then dimmed in Mark's hand. Time to get a new flashlight? Maybe not, keep reading.

In the meantime, the spirit box continued to spit out many single-syllable sounds. We tend to discount these because they're too easy to misinterpret. We shut it off and began an audio-only recording session. Mark asked if someone was manipulating the flashlight – never hurts to ask. Of course, we didn't hear a response until we analyzed our recordings later.

Here's that exciting EVP we mentioned earlier. In playback, we heard Mark's question, followed by an immediate reply of "Yes" in a woman's voice. (Remember that this occurred in Maud's room.) The event may not *sound* too impressive, but getting a voice using nothing but an audio-only tape recording is gold during paranormal investigations, ranking just below an apparition on videotape. Our recording produced one of the clearest EVPs from an audio-only session we'd captured to date. In fact, it was so clear, the voice required no audio-editing at all for us to hear. (We did boost the amplitude slightly for our YouTube documentation.)

In Room 209, we captured one of our clearest EVPs.

That event excited us to analyze the spirit box session. To our surprise (in real time, we didn't think we'd captured much at all), the recording revealed several intelligible phrases just after we turned on the spirit box. They included spirits saying, "Here it is" and "Wait please." Coinciding with the flashlight episode, we also recorded "[something]'s broke." We couldn't quite make out that first word. All these statements came in a man's voice – ironic, since our audio-only session recorded a woman's voice.

Luckily, we managed to capture the flashlight episode in Room 209 on video and Maud's response to that event on audio recording.

The investigation continued across the hall in Room 210,

where housekeeping had reported moving clothes hangers and electrical anomalies. EMF baselines produced readings of 530-590mG around the room, with the bed showing 630-670mG (bedsprings again?)

The real-time spirit box greeted us with "Hi, Kym." When we asked how many spirits joined us in the room, we heard an unequivocal "Two." The flashlight performed perfectly this time – but also without results.

During later analysis, we had what sounded like another audio-only EVP, but we couldn't tease out the words. On the spirit box recording, the same woman again greeted us with "Hi, Kym," adding the word "Lucy" to our request for who was with us. When we requested further communication, a man's voice answered, "Did we?" But when we asked for flashlight manipulation, a woman's voice told us, "I'm so sorry." Finally, we asked if they had any questions for us and heard, "Hold on, Mark (woman's voice), Kym (man's voice)."

We did hold on but, alas, no one offered anything further.

Couldn't really complain, though – the investigation had already yielded very productive results.

Highlights of the Area

Enjoy a variety of outdoor activities here, including hiking, biking, fishing, and more. The Rio Grande River promises plenty of hungry brown trout to add to your fish stories. At Del Norte, visitors can escape the fast lane and find four seasons of fun and activities.

Del Norte Chamber of Commerce
PO Box 372, Del Norte, CO 81132
(719) 657-9081
delnortechamber.org

Monte Vista Chamber of Commerce
947 1st Ave., Monte Vista, CO 81144
(719) 852-2731
monte-vista.org

Annual Festivals
- Monte Vista Crane Festival – March
- Pagosa Springs Music Festivals – June & September
- Covered Wagon Days – July/August

Cultural/Recreational Opportunities
- Del Norte Trails
  Scenic system of trails for hikers, bicyclers, horseback riders
  PO Box 255, Del Norte, CO
  delnortetrails.org

- Diamond-D-Bar Ranch & Outfitters
  Hunting, cattle drives, fishing, pack trips
  8018 N Rd 6 West, Del Norte, CO
  (719) 850-1722
  diamond-d-bar-outfitters.com

- Great Sand Dunes National Park
  Tallest dunes in America
  11999 Highway 150 Mosca, CO
  719-378-6399
  nps.gov/grsa/index.htm

- Penitente Canyon
  Rock Climbing
  County Road 38A, Del Norte, CO
  (719) 852-5941
  fs.usda.gov/recarea/riogrande/recarea/?recid=64790
- Rio Grande County Museum

Cultural and natural history of the San Luis Valley
580 Oak Street, Del Norte, CO
(719) 657-2847
museumtrail.org/RioGrandeCountyMuseum.asp

- San Juan National Forest
Nearly 2 million acres of public land
(970) 247-4874
fs.usda.gov/sanjuan

More
- Colorado's Rio Grande Country
riograndecountry.com

Chapter Five
Delta

Fairlamb House B&B

Fairlamb House B&B

700 Leon St, Delta, CO 81416
(970) 874-5158
fairlambbb.com

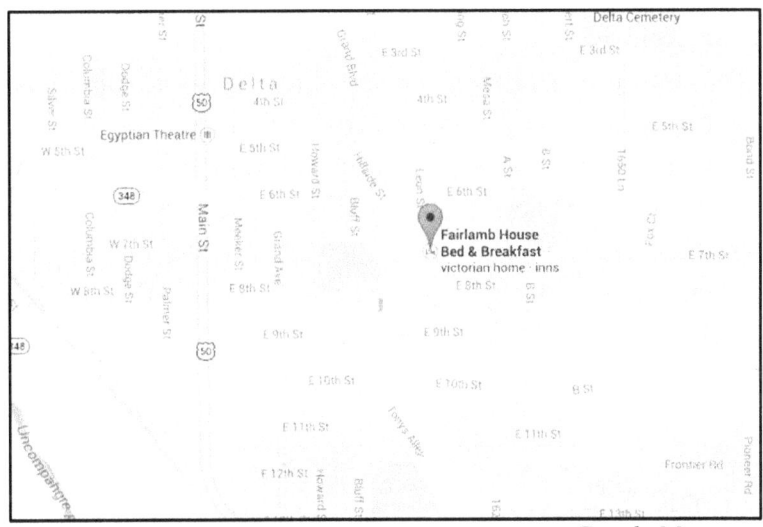

Google Map

Season: Year round
Peak: Summer months
Pet friendly: Yes
Family friendly: Best suited for older children
WiFi: Yes

DESCRIPTION, AMBIENCE, FURNISHINGS

Approaching the front porch to the Fairlamb House feels like stepping into a post-Victorian world. The building's façade windows display antique soldered decorative panes, and the front door lets in light through an oval of beveled glass – all of period construction.

The entryway and foyer contain original inlaid floors using two patterns and a combination of four different hardwoods.

Once inside, the first-floor layout follows the plan of a stately turn-of-the-century home: open staircase straight ahead, library and reading room to the right, and parlor to the left. A dining room and attached kitchen sits off the parlor. Hardwood floors, oriental rugs and heavy, comfortable furniture fill all the rooms as well as period decorations, potted plants, and rich woodwork.

The entryway opens before a grandfather clock and open staircase leading to the guestrooms.

Wandering around the first floor is a visual treat with its multitude of antiques. A handmade grandfather clock stands next to the open staircase; a lovely old upright pump organ takes up one corner of the library next to a Tiffany floor lamp; a laced-curtain bay window fills the dining room with light. Everywhere you look, you'll see reminders of an affluent bygone era.

The old pump organ accents the library, once Millard Fairlamb's business office.

The B&B's parlor and breakfast room offers period décor.

The second floor contains three guest rooms as well as a sitting area and two bathrooms, one featuring a porcelain claw-footed tub. All rooms uniquely reflect the decorative style of the day, complete with antiques and family heirlooms.

The Millard Room appears masculine with darker and heavier accents, an oval-mirrored wooden wardrobe, and a black-and-gold wrought-iron bedstand. Lighter colors characterize the Stella Room, with white wrought iron, pastel print wallpaper, and a display case holding decorative Victorian purses. Decidedly feminine describes the Ethel Room, with its canopy brass bed and gown-bedecked mannequins.

One interesting tidbit about the Ethel Room: what is now a garment closet was once a connecting passageway to the adjoining bedroom (now a personal office). This passageway offered discrete access from one room to the other, designed for conjugal visits – thus the name "discretion closet," which was common in Victorian homes.

The B&B provides robes for each guest and a locked unit for bicycles and motorcycles. A garden patio caters to smoking guests.

Past and Present

For hundreds of years, this area was homelands to the Ute tribes, and by the early 1800s, a trading post sprang up in the region to serve Native Americans, traders, and trappers. In 1828, Antoine Robidoux built Fort Uncompahgre, established as a fur trading center. The nearby 200-year old Ute Council Tree still commemorates the tribe's Chief Ouray and his wife Chipeta. Legend says Chipeta was the only Ute woman ever permitted to sit in council meetings held at this site.

Millard and Stella Fairlamb built the house in 1906. Millard kept a Utah desert skeleton for years in the house's attic.

Delta County was created by the Colorado legislature in 1883. The town took its name from the delta that forms at the confluence of the Uncompahgre and Gunnison rivers. The area's story reflects a heritage of pioneering agriculture, mining, land and water development.

Millard and Stella Fairlamb built The Fairlamb House in 1906, constructed of local Delta brick in classic Four Square architectural style. It was the first home in the area built by workers on an eight-hour work day. The house stood on a bluff that overlooked the delta below, and family members erected a series of houses that stretched an entire block. The Fairlamb House is listed on the State Historical Register.

One curious story revolves around Millard, who combed through the nearby Utah desert in search of Indian artifacts. Finding a human skeleton, he gathered up the bones, put them in a box, and stored them in his third-floor attic. There they stayed for a number of years, always scaring the Fairlamb children. Eventually, the skeleton was turned over to the Utes for interment.

The house passed from Millard and Stella to Charles and Ethel Fairlamb and later Harley and Ethel (Lale) Fairlamb Jackson, and it continued to stay in the family for over seventy-two years. The Fairlambs experienced their share of life's tragedies, including the death of one household member after she fell from a ladder hanging Christmas lights. After 1978, the house continued under two subsequent owners, both doctors, and also numerous renters.

John Taylor and Elizabeth Thompson purchased the house in 1994, and they've maintained the turn-of-the-century décor.

LEGENDS, STORIES, AND GUEST EXPERIENCES

Despite the fact that there was a skeleton in the attic for years and at least one Fairlamb family member died on the premises, current B&B owners John and Elizabeth attest they've personally witnessed very few instances of paranormal activity other than the occasional odd noises that an old house can make.

Elizabeth did, however, experience an unexplained phenomenon during the renovations. She'd hired a high school girl to help, and soon the student pointed out a small seashell placed on a shelf kept showing up in other parts of the house. At first, Elizabeth thought the girl was playing a joke on her. But when she started paying attention, she, too, noticed the rogue seashell popping up in strange places.

Then in 1996, two years after the new owners purchased the property, they learned five female spirits resided at the Fairlamb. During the Ute powwow that year, the B&B played host to several visiting Native Americans, including a Lakota medicine man and his wife. That first morning at breakfast, the couple told John and Elizabeth they'd almost left in the middle of the night because of what happened to them. The medicine man recounted they both woke to five benevolent female spirits standing at the foot of their bed in the Millard Room. They told the shaman they were trapped in the house.

The Lakota offered to perform a release ceremony, which included chanting and burning sage that he wafted with an eagle feather. The ceremony may have released those five trapped ghosts, but paranormal activity continued for at least one woman we interviewed, who regularly stays at the Fairlamb.

A year after the Lakotas visited, she reported seeing a wicker chair rocking on its own in the bathroom while she washed her face. She again stayed at the house in 2001 with her husband and baby. Back in the same bathroom, lights started to flicker and she heard banging noises. On a third visit, nothing paranormal occurred to her, but she still sensed an unseen presence – even when alone in the house.

OUR PERSONAL EXPERIENCES

We were a little nervous about what ghosts remained in the house after the medicine man's release ceremony. We needn't have been.

Because the five women spirits had been reported in the Millard Room, we chose to start our investigation there. Baseline EMFs fell in the 510mG range near the bed and slightly lower everywhere else in the room. Our spirit box went so crazy with squelching feedback that we heard very little in real time. We recorded with the spirit box for only a short while and resorted to straight audio recording to see if we could detect any EVPs later.

Guests witnessed the simultaneous appearance of five women spirits in the Millard Room

More interesting during the real-time spirit box session, our flashlight flickered immediately after we asked spirits to dim the 160-lumen light. Simultaneously, the EMF meter increased by

160mG. We documented the dimming of the light on video. The correlation of request, dimming, and EMF fluctuation was striking, and confirmed the willingness of an unseen presence or presences to interact with us.

Later spirit box analysis drew responses to our question about who was there, giving the names "Hutch" three times (in a man's voice), and "Wilhelm" once (in a woman's voice). The spirit box also produced a man's voice saying, "Girls," and a different man's voice saying, "Crappy" – as though expressing an opinion. When we'd asked whether the entities in the B&B preferred the term "Ghosts" or "Spirits," we got immediate responses, including a boy's voice twice saying, "Ghosts." During our investigations, we've seldom recorded children's voices.

On audio-only recording analysis, we picked up the EVP of a feminine whisper of "Help me, Kym." Messages like this tend to frustrate us since we only hear them in analysis, long after we've left the premises.

The Stella Room, where we may have spoken to "Thelma"

Across the hall in the Stella Room, our EMF baselines were 480mG in the north end of the room, 530mG in the south, and

570mG over the bed. Again, our spirit box suffered from a fair amount of reverberation. The only thing we clearly heard in real time was a woman's voice saying, "Home … yes" in response to our query asking if this was any spirit's home. We could also make out the word "Four" when we asked how many spirits were present. We expected an answer of five, based on the other guests' reports, but we hardly felt disappointed!

We captured those same words again when we later analyzed the session, and when we listened to ourselves thanking the woman for her response, she said, "Okay." At this point in our session, we'd again turned on the flashlight and asked for interaction. Nothing happened. Perhaps because a woman's voice reported, "Problems." We also asked her name, to which she answered, "Thelma." Then we asked if she'd died there, and she answered "yes." (We found no reference to a historical record of a Thelma dying on the premises.)

When we asked where the spirits were now, one man's voice commanded, "Answer!" followed by a different man saying, "Here." We inquired about the bones in the attic, to which a woman replied, "We're dead."

The audio-only recording in that room produced no later EVPs. Same thing with the video analysis.

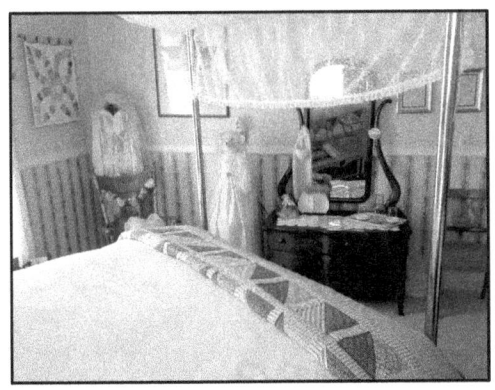

The Ethel Room lies directly below the location in the attic where Fairlamb stored a skeleton. We captured an EVP of "bones" multiple times in this room.

We concluded our investigation with sessions in the remaining Ethel Room. EMF readings fluctuated only slightly from 470-480mG throughout the room. When we again tried the flashlight experiment, the EMF rose to 610mG, but the light didn't dim or flutter. Later in the session, our camcorder shut down, still with a three-quarters full battery. (More on that later.)

Puzzling, but we had no reverberations on the spirit box like we'd experienced in the other rooms. In fact, within seconds we heard the word "bones" repeated three times. We asked whose bones, and a man's voice said, "Wife." We also heard the words "Blood," "Death," and "Company."

On analysis, we detected the same words we had in real time, along with a number of others. During the flashlight request, a woman's voice said, "It's a thing – thing." A reference to the flashlight? Right after that, another woman's voice asked, "Who's there? Hello?" We asked for another sign of spirit presence, and two different men repeated what the boy said earlier: "ghosts." At the same real-time moment the camcorder shut down, we discovered later that nothing recorded on video – even though it seemed to be running. On the analysis, at that timeframe a woman's disgusted voice announced, "That's it" (emphasis on "that"). The separate audio-only recording gave us nothing.

We may not have made contact with the original five women spirits in the house, but we certainly got a dismissal from someone.

Highlights of the Area

Expect plenty of amenities in this charming Colorado town, including grassy city parks as well as murals depicting the local economy, history, and natural surroundings. Real western hospitality complements a broad scope of recreational and cultural opportunities.

Delta Chamber of Commerce
301 Main St., Delta, CO 81416
(970) 874-8616
deltacolorado.org

Annual Festivals
- Dragon Unchained Festival and Faire – April
- Deltarado Days – July
- Olathe Sweetcorn Festival – August
- Council Tree Pow Wow – September

Cultural/Recreational Opportunities
- Black Canyon of the Gunnison
  Some of the steepest cliffs and oldest rock in the U.S.
  Montrose/Gunnison, CO
  (970) 641-2337
  nps.gov/blca

- Black Canyon Wing & Clay
  Clay target range
  2566 Last Chance Rd., Delta, CO
  (970) 874-7195
  bcwandc.com

- City of Delta Parks
  List of local parks
  Delta, CO

(970) 874-7973
delta-co.gov/parks.html

- Delta County Museum
  Local historical artifacts
  251 Meeker St., Delta, CO
  (970) 874-8721
  swcoloradoheritage.com/heritage-attractions/delta-county-museum

- Dominguez-Escalante National Conservation Area
  Bureau of Land Management scenic and wildlife area
  2815 H Rd., Grand Junction, CO
  (970) 244-3000
  blm.gov/co/st/en/nca/denca.html

- Montrose County Historical Museum
  Historical artifacts from the area
  21 North Rio Grande, Montrose, CO
  (970) 249-2085
  montrosehistory.org

- Museum of the Mountain West
  Historic memorabilia and buildings
  68169 Miami Rd., Montrose, CO
  (970) 240-3400
  museumofthemountainwest.org

- Sweitzer Lake
  Fishing, water sports
  Delta, CO
  (970) 874-4258
  cpw.state.co.us/placestogo/Parks/sweitzerlake

- Ute Indian Museum
  History of the Ute tribe
  17253 Chipeta Dr., Montrose, CO
  (970) 249-3098
  historycolorado.org/museums/ute-indian-museum-0

More
- Delta County, Colorado
  deltacountycolorado.com

- Visit Montrose
  visitmontrose.com

Chapter Six
Fairplay

Fairplay Hotel

Fairplay Hotel

500 Main Street, Fairplay CO 80440
(719) 836-4699
fairplayhotelco.com

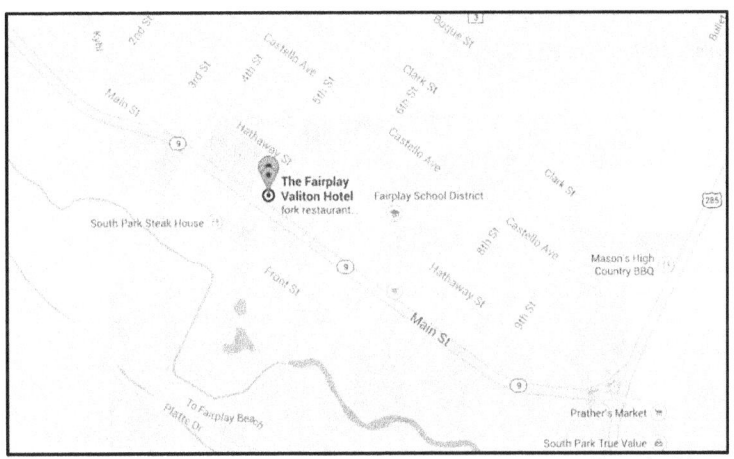

Google Map

Season: Year round
Peak: Summer months
Pet friendly: Yes
Family friendly: Yes
WiFi: Yes

Description, Ambience, Furnishings

The Fairplay Hotel has an Old West exterior that carries into the lobby and rooms we saw. Once inside, the spacious lobby sports a large stone fireplace, comfortable period furnishings, and chandeliered high ceilings supported by dark-wood boxed beams. Old-timey wainscoting accents the reception area, hallways, and dining room, visible as you step through the lobby door. The décor includes authentic hardwood floors, and historic photos and plaques decorate the walls.

The hotel lobby features Western décor.

The effect is warm and welcoming, just like the hotel staff.

The in-house restaurant offers an upscale appearance with black linen tablecloths and interesting turn-of-the-century pictures and vases. Lunch and dinner specials accompany a broader menu that caters to locals and travelers alike.

*The hotel dining room
is open to public and guests.*

French doors adjoin Gatsby's Restaurant and River Roxx Bar. The massive wooden bar and stools in the lounge originally belonged to "Silver Heels," a late 1800s brothel madam in the nearby frontier mining town of Alma. Adding to the frontier ambience is an old bullet hole on one end of the back bar, left from that rowdier era. Just past the lounge, doors lead into a dance room, newly remodeled and featuring regular live bands.

Up the two-flight staircase, travelers enter intersecting hallways that connect to large guest rooms, comfortably accommodating four or more people and nicely furnished with antique beds and dressers. Unlike bygone days, each room has its own private bath and modern conveniences such as WiFi.

The hotel regularly plays host to a number of festive events, including Halloween and Victorian costume balls and a New Year's Eve party. The building also provides a banquet room for private, catered parties.

New owner Lorna Arnold took the helm in the summer of 2014 and continues to renovate and upgrade the building.

Past and Present

Prior to the influx of gold seekers, the First Americans, primarily Ute tribes, lived and hunted in the South Park area. Fur traders found and trapped the park, but it wasn't until 1859 that the Pike's Peak Gold Rush spilled into South Park, bringing more than 10,000 people.

Greed and violence in the park prompted some miners to establish a new camp where Beaver Creek meets the Middle Fork of the South Platte River. They called their new home "Fair Play," promising to treat everyone fairly when they staked a claim. That name varied from "Fairplay Diggings" to "Platte City" and then changed to "South Park City" by 1869. But five years later, the town regained the name of "Fairplay," which remains to this day.

Before long, cattle, sheep, and hay operations came to the park, followed by a railroad completed in 1878. The railway encouraged the emergence of timber businesses and more efficient livestock transport. Soon, other trades, goods, and services prospered, making it possible for local hotels to flourish in Fairplay.

Among these new innkeepers were Louis and Marie Valiton, who bought a site in 1873 for $87.50 and built the Valiton Hotel (now the Fairplay Hotel). During the Gold Rush days, Fairplay still had its share of Wild West antics, and the hotel's basement until recent years still contained tunnels connecting to other buildings – a more subtle way to access the hotel's ladies of the evening. Current owner Lorna told us, "Back then, you could rent a room and a woman." One of these tunnels led to the old courthouse due north of the hotel, and the site of a vigilante lynching in 1879 by a group calling themselves the "Hundred and Five" and daring anyone to oppose their style of justice.

Silver Heels held a license for prostitution, now displayed at the hotel.

A now collapsed tunnel once connected the courthouse and jail to the hotel.

    The local newspaper, *The Fairplay Flume*, printed one of their messages, which read, "Beware the vigilantes," and signed the letter "Coffin." Eventually, law and order returned to the community.

    Like the town itself, the Valiton Hotel's name went through a number of changes over the next forty years as new owners left their marks, including the McLain Hotel, the Vestal House, the Bergh House, the Fairplay Hotel, and Hotel Windsor. The Hotel Windsor survived one large fire throughout town but suffered enough from a second town-wide fire to close its doors in 1921. Prominent Park County citizens rebuilt the establishment on the remaining foundation using the original hotel floor plans, and the new facility opened in 1922 with a banquet and dance hall.

With Prohibition's repeal in 1934, the hotel relocated the mahogany back bar from Rachel's Place, a famous saloon in nearby Alma, and the new lounge has become a favorite among Fairplay locals ever since.

Because of the building's large hospitality spaces, community members continued to use the facilities for celebrations and meetings through the decades that followed.

Restorations still preserve the historic flavor of the premises under current management.

Legends, Stories, and Guest Experiences

Many stories of hauntings and paranormal activity have persisted through the hotel's colorful history over the past century.

Two staff members have reported seeing full apparitions on separate occasions in the basement. In fact, the chef had his own encounter late one night after closing. Ascending from the basement, he heard footsteps above him on the stairs just beyond the landing to the second flight of steps. No one else was on the premises. When he returned to the first floor minutes later, all the lights were off on the main level.

One staff person on another evening saw a cowboy in old-fashioned western attire just outside the lounge peer in through the window. When she went out the door to the deck to invite him in, no one was there. Only a few seconds had passed – too little time for anyone to disappear or retreat from view on the empty street outside.

We interviewed paranormal investigator Shaun Crusha, who set up motion sensors and laser grids along the tables in the River Roxx bar, and he documented on camcorder a sequence of invisible movement that traversed the length of the bar.

Lorna told us that when she took possession of the hotel, she placed a half-full glass of beer in front of the barstool favored by Silver Heels, the brothel madam from Alma, when the Fairplay Hotel relocated the bar to their own lounge. They locked the doors and left for the night. The next morning, they found the glass empty, with the barstool swiveled away as though someone had stood up after finishing the drink.

Silver Heels' favorite stool sits below the bullet hole in the River Roxx back bar.

A note on Silver Heels: This good-hearted and popular prostitute worked the mining camps northwest of Fairplay until the smallpox epidemic of 1861 invaded the area. She went from cabin to cabin nursing sick miners but succumbed herself to the disfiguring disease and later disappeared without a trace. Years later, some said a heavily veiled woman frequented a nearby cemetery, and they guessed she might have been Silver Heels.

She may have never left. Several locals claim to have seen the apparition of a veiled woman dressed in black and wandering the cemetery with flowers in her hand. It's possible she followed her bar furnishings to the Fairplay Hotel, where her framed license for prostitution is displayed on a wall, issued in 1884 at Fairplay.

The hotel's most famous and recurring ghost is "Julia," reported to have died by her own hand in the 1880s. Guests often hear her dancing down the second-floor hallways, sometimes hearing music to match her creaking steps on the hardwood floors. Occasionally, the key to her room goes missing. It was curious that the night before we arrived for our investigation, someone had requested her room (205), but no one could find the key so they couldn't rent out the room.

Prostitute "Julia" allegedly committed suicide, and her ghost now dances at night in the second-floor hallways.

OUR PERSONAL EXPERIENCES

Lucky for us, the hotel let us set up in one of Julia's old, ahem, *haunts* – Room 205. In fact, the spirit seemed to insist. (See previous section.). Guess she was waiting for us.

In her room, we used our array of ghost-hunting gizmos to see if we could establish her presence – spirit box, EMF meter, digital recorder, and video camera.

Right off, the spirit box went crazy, spitting out multiple words that described the room, interspersed with observations about our various activities ("Room," "Bed," "Shower" as well as "Videotape," while we recorded). We also got two instances of "Knife" – a reference to how Julia died? The box declared a number of unconfirmed names that might be related to the history of the place, including "Daniel" and "Sarah" twice as well as "Joseph," "Barbara," "Rachel," "Jennifer," and "Linda." We weren't sure who we were talking to.

In fact, the spirit box was so noisy we finally turned it off to concentrate on audio-only EVP recordings. When we afterward analyzed these results, at the moment Mark invited her to talk to us during the sessions, we found a whispered response that sounded like "I don't want to talk to you." But when we teased this one out using audio-editing software, we discovered the woman's voice had actually said, "I don't want to f**k with you"! Guess Mark wasn't her type. Nonetheless, this EVP excited us because such recordings are so rare – and it was a complete sentence in response to our query.

Moving on to EMF readings, we found a consistent baseline of 196-225mG. That level didn't change much throughout the suite … until Kym's meter started to spike close to 700mG near the north bed of the two in the bedroom. It also spiked over the chair between the beds. Soon, Kym's meter sounded alarms from those two spots, suggesting goings-on we couldn't see.

We ran video in Julia's room, but none of the tape revealed more than we could see with our own eyes.

After checking out the hallways to detect Julia's dancing (not while we visited), we headed down to the lounge. There we found a patron staking out Silver Heel's haunted stool. He kindly stepped aside when we asked to take a photograph. He joked about the infamous stool, claiming he'd never seen a feminine spirit while he sat there. Too much activity in the lounge prevented us from taking readings or conducting an EVP session, but we thought the bullet hole in the bar's polished wood looked pretty cool.

Before lunch, we headed down to the basement, amused that someone pointed to the entrance and said, "There it is." He didn't offer to accompany us any further. Narrow red-tile risers led us down one flight to a landing that turned sharply to the left and ended at the mouth of the basement. We found the switch for the two lonely light bulbs and snapped them on. Shadowed masonry and odd little cubby holes hid much of the closed tunnels that had once led to the nearby courthouse and other buildings. The noise of the restaurant and kitchen above us again prevented taking any readings. One little cubicle with no light bulb held a single chair, giving us pause to wonder who used that as a sitting room.

We decided to go back upstairs and order lunch in Gatsby's Restaurant. While we munched on chicken enchiladas (scrumptious, by the way), Kym *almost* saw a ghost – a cowboy sauntering on the other side of the lace-curtained windows of the adjoining lounge. Then he seemed to disappear. The staff's cowboy specter? No such luck: he turned out to be flesh-n-blood and had turned toward a bar stool she couldn't see.

Maybe next time.

The Hand Hotel

Hand Hotel Bed & Breakfast

531 Front Street, Fairplay, CO 80440
(719) 836-3595
HandHotel.com

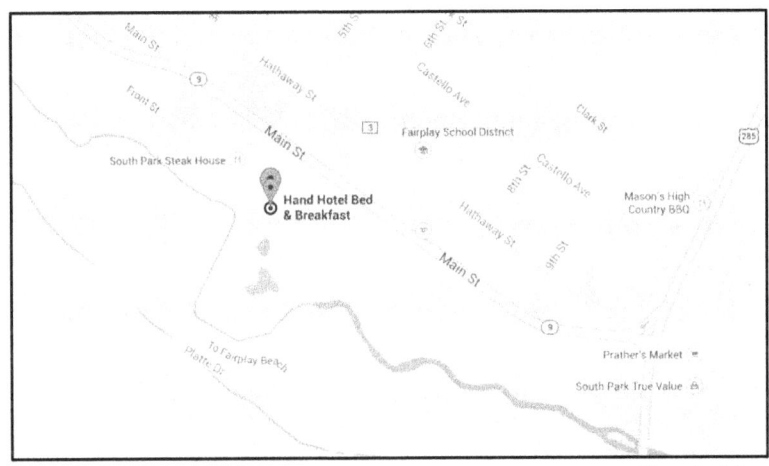

Google Map

Season: Year round
Peak: April to October
Pet friendly: Yes ($5/night extra)
Family friendly: Yes
WiFi: Yes

DESCRIPTION, AMBIENCE, FURNISHINGS

The rustic, rough-board exterior of the Hand Hotel Bed and Breakfast looks deceiving compared to the warmth and charm within. Expect the first host you see to have long ears and antlers – the elk mounted over the registration desk. Depending on the time of year, he'll wear a baseball cap, Christmas ornaments, or other seasonal baubles. Turn your head to the right and you'll notice a plaque over the dining room doorway proclaiming, "On This Site in 1897 Nothing Happened."

Clearly, this is a hotel with a sense of humor.

Depending on the season, different decorations adorn the elk over the registration desk.

A gift shop and a craft shop flank both sides of the lobby.

A large rock fireplace adorns a hardwood-floor lobby decorated with Persian rug, oversized furniture, and antler chandelier. The entire space displays the types of wall hangings you'd expect to see a hundred years ago in an upscale hunting lodge, including a furry animal hide tacked over period wallpaper.

On either side of the entrance, two souvenir gift shops – one with Victorian and the other with western motif – sell clothing and home decorating bric-a-brac.

Beyond the lobby an open doorway leads to a cozy breakfast area with multiple tables for four and the floor covered with turn-of-the-century floral-pattered carpet. Keep walking and you step down into a lovely picture-window solarium overlooking the Platte River. Greenery and flower blossoms complement a breathtaking view of water, forest, and mountains.

The hotel offers a continental breakfast.

The enclosed solarium overlooks the South Platte River.

From the reception area, a staircase turns on one landing to lead to the second floor of eleven guest rooms, themed with such names as The Miner, The Trapper, The Outlaw, and Grandma Hand – all featuring private baths and a variety of bed sizes. All the rooms hold antique furnishings that offer a feel for a luxurious version of yesteryear.

Both ends of the upstairs hallway open to balconies, the front overlooking Fairplay's business district and the back a second-floor view toward the Platte and high Rocky Mountains shouldering the west side of South Park.

Past and Present

The town of Fairplay lies within the high, broad South Park valley, stretching over 900 square miles bordered by the Mosquito and Park mountain ranges.

Ute tribes summered in the region, and eventually French trappers arrived to hunt and trade in furs. By the mid-1800s, cattle and sheep operations moved in, but it was the discovery of gold in South Park in 1859 that brought large numbers of eager miners and the development of camps and towns like Fairplay.

A prospering mining industry encouraged migration to the South Park area, followed by permanent settlements. As more people moved in, the community demanded such skilled services as carpentry and blacksmithing. Wagon roads gave way to narrow gauge railways, and soon entrepreneurs provided dance halls, saloons, and gambling houses.

A fire ravaged Fairplay in the 1920s, destroying much of the town, including the building on Front Street where the Hand Hotel now stands. The Hand family built this new structure in 1932, and it stayed in their family for many years. Decades later, however, the hotel became abandoned and condemned, so rundown that the sky shone through the roof. Pat Pocius and two partners purchased the building in 1987 and began massive renovations. She ran the new hotel for the next decade. The hotel changed hands again in the late 1990s and eventually came under the current ownership of Dale and Kathy Fitting.

Next to the Hand Hotel stands the monument and grave of "Prunes," a burro that worked in the mines for sixty-two years. He turned into something of a town pet when he became too old to work. The burro's life-long (human) partner, Rupe Sherwood, requested he be cremated and buried beside Prunes when he died. The annual Burro Days celebrates the important role burros played during the mining era. Each July, burro races start on Front Street near Prunes' monument.

The monument to "Prunes"

Legends, Stories, and Guest Experiences

The Hand Hotel has a fair amount of paranormal activity, with reports of full-body apparitions manifesting on the second-floor hallway, faces appearing on at least one guestroom mirror, and child-size imprints on freshly made beds. Housekeeping staff often find messed-up beds after they've prepared and locked rooms. The hotel reputedly hosts five different ghosts.

A guest took this reproduced photo on the second floor, but apparitions reportedly walk throughout the hotel.

One of the daytime receptionists said she thinks multiple ghosts roam through the building. She once saw an apparition standing at the window in Room Six as she walked past the open doorway. She could see through the shadowy figure, but it was gone when she stopped to take another peek back into the room.

Former hotel owner Pat Pocius shared several encounters, most notably with two little girls who haunt the building. They reportedly died during a smallpox epidemic in an earlier era in Fairplay. Occasionally seen near the staircase, the girls also made their presence known in the kitchen, repeatedly turning off the heavy knob pilots on the commercial grill during a busy morning. When Pat investigated the wiring underneath, she discovered charred receptacles that could have started a fire. She felt sure the girls were doing their part to avoid catastrophe.

Pat also recounted the time when a friend came to visit and wanted to see the second-floor rooms. Pat was busy and let her friend wander around on her own. The friend encountered an older man pushing a cart down the hallway and who told her his name was Ben and to call him if she needed anything. When she returned downstairs, she complimented Pat on the courteous staff. There were no staff in the building that day, but Ben was the name of the former hotel caretaker, dead many years.

Our favorite paranormal sighting, though, is about the ghost dog, which roams the entire premises. Rooms Two and Eleven have many reports of guests inquiring about who's keeping a dog at the hotel – but it's not there for a one-time visit! On one occasion, a town constable emerged from the downstairs bathroom with pants still around his knees, complaining about a dog that had chased him out. No one could find a dog in the facilities afterwards.

The ghost dog also has a reputation for appearing in various rooms and tugging bedcovers off guests during the night, sometimes barking or growling. Another account occurred in the basement which, at the time, was the site for a children's Halloween party. Two tykes came upstairs, reporting they enjoyed playing with the dog in the basement. Pat said she could see the imprints on their little hands, looking like a puppy had playfully nipped them.

There are also reports of feet tramping on the second-floor ceiling. Pat remarked guests have often inquired how to get to the party on the third floor. There is no third floor.

Other poltergeist activity also occurs. The wife of a previous hotel manager twice smelled the scent of rosewater perfume in the Grandma Hand Room. The wife later learned that was the very scent Grandma Hand used to wear.

Our Personal Experiences

We took our cue from a scrapbook reporting on guest accounts of the hotel's paranormal happenings – plus the receptionist's experiences – and decided to set up our base of operations in Room Six, which displayed a door faceplate called "Mattie Silks." This infamous lady of the night hailed from the Front Range in the late Nineteenth Century and may have had enterprises in Fairplay. The room's furnishings reflected typical brothel décor with lavish red wallpaper, brass bed, and several mirrors.

The Mattie Silks Room, where a hotel staffer saw an apparition at the window

We wanted that room because of the staff sighting of a semi-transparent apparition standing just inside the windowpanes. Room Six was also near one end of the hallway, which gave us a quiet place to conduct our investigation.

Kym scouted out the premises while Mark set up to record audio for possible EVPs. Later analysis revealed two sequences of voices on the recording, following Mark's requests for interaction. Both were clearly of the same woman with a lilting voice, but neither one of us could make out exactly what she said. Kym's impression was she spoke the word "Baby" in the utterance. Not an unlikely reference for a room named after a brothel madam or the life of soiled doves who worked the brothels in that era.

In the meantime, Kym had chatted up another guest out on the balcony, a woman who'd visited the Hand Hotel on three separate occasions. She told Kym that each room she'd tried had a different personality, and she suggested we look in the one near the head of the stairs on the second floor.

We trotted down to the other room – unoccupied, door open – and ... yes, it definitely had a different vibe. Was it due to a resident ghost or just the room's distinct décor? The receptionist assured us the hotel ghosts wandered promiscuously (our word, not hers) from room to room, so maybe the impression was just ours. And the other guest's.

Back in our own room, the spirit box seemed fixated on "Table," which it repeated a number of times. There were two small tables located in the room, but we couldn't detect if one was more significant than the other. No orbs appeared on photographs, and the EMF meter didn't spike near either of the tables. The meter did, however, climb when Kym sat on the brass bed. Base readings in the room in general hovered near 300mG compared to the bed, which jumped to 500+ mG intermittently during our investigation.

We also set up our video camera in the room, pointing it at the infamous window and letting it run while we conducted spirit box and EVP sessions. Review of the footage revealed no further anomalies. (To be fair, the videocam had to battle a fair amount of outside window glare.) In retrospect, we wish we had set it up for a while in the shotgun hallway outside the door, where other guests had reported so much activity. That day we also didn't get much of a jump beyond the baseline EMF readings in that corridor of the hotel. That's certainly the location of the great photo of the apparition included in this account.

Overall, our room had a warm and inviting ambiance – despite the reported brooding apparition at the window.

We asked to visit the basement but learned it was off-limits except to employees. That was okay with us since we preferred not to be bitten by the ghost dog.

Our own experience suggests, to paraphrase the staff, that the local ghost residents decided not to play with us as much as they often do with other guests. But we'd like to give this hotel another visit sometime – too much going on here not to!

Highlights of the Area

Surrounded by majestic peaks and pastoral splendor, Fairplay hosts colorful festivals and events, combining a mining heritage with its quaint mountain character. Ghost towns, gold panning areas, fishing holes, hiking trails, and snowmobiling terrain make this a recreational paradise year round.

South Park Chamber of Commerce
P.O. Box 312, Fairplay, CO 80440
(719) 836-3410
southparkchamber.com

Annual Festivals
- Burro Days – July
- Festival in the Clouds (Alma) – July
- Independence Day Celebration – July
- Ladies Run of Colorado – July
- Race in the Clouds (Alma bike races) – July
- South Park Music Festival – July
- South Park Bead & Fiber Show – August
- South Park Arts Celebration – September

Cultural/Recreational Opportunities
- High Creek Fen Preserve
  Thriving wetlands open to the public
  Fairplay, CO
  (303) 444-2950
  nature.org/ourinitiatives/regions/northamerica/unitedstates/colorado/placesweprotect/high-creek-fen-preserve.xml

- Pike and San Isabel National Forests
  Wilderness areas and outdoor opportunities
  Fairplay vicinity, CO
  (719) 553-1400
  fs.usda.gov/psicc

- South Park City
  Open-air museum
  100 4th St., Fairplay, CO
  (719) 836-2387
  southparkcity.org

- South Park National Heritage Area
  Heritage, history, resources
  P.O. Box 1373, Fairplay, CO
  (719) 836-4273
  southparkheritage.org

- South Park Recreation Center
  Pool, sauna, weight room
  1190 Bullet Rd., Fairplay, CO
  (719) 836-0747
  southparkrec.org

More
- Town of Fairplay
  fairplayco.us

Chapter Seven
Gunnison

Photo by Beth Marcue

Vintage Inn B&B

Vintage Inn B&B

123 N. Boulevard St., Gunnison, CO 81230
(970) 596-1848
VintageInnGunnison.com

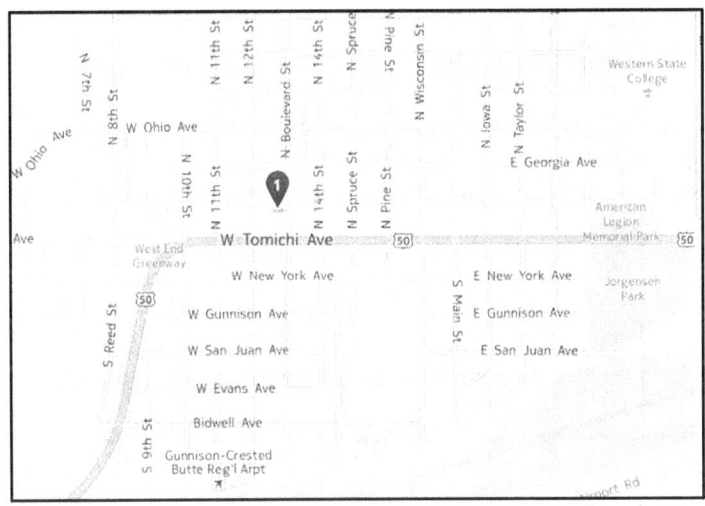

Google Map

Season: Year round
Peak: April through October
Pet friendly: Yes
Family friendly: Yes
WiFi: Yes

Description, Ambience, Furnishings

The Vintage Inn preserves the charming Victorian character and style of an 1880s home – period mauve-painted clapboard siding, intricate detail on all the trim and outside window moldings, covered porches, and scalloped braces beneath the overhang of the roof eaves.

Artist Beth Marcue opened the B&B in 2010.

This one-story structure is deceptively roomy inside. Oriental rugs complement the hardwood floors and heavy furniture. Several of the interior doors feature arched corners, perhaps the remnants of what were once exterior doors. The house has undergone multiple renovations since Civil-War Capt. Louden Mullins constructed it as his home. But many of the windows retain the original glass.

The B&B owner, Beth Marcue, works as an artist, and it shows in the house's décor. Walls and tables display a wide variety of eclectic effects using original paintings, sculpture, and collectible *objets d'art*.

A cozy hearth room takes center stage in the house, connecting kitchen and living room – all available to overnight guests.

The Hearth Room offers a cozy mix of period furnishings and unique art.

Note the arches of the doorway frame, a remnant of the original architecture.

The B&B offers a single, spacious guestroom with *en-suite* private bath, suitable for a couple and even space for a child. Beth has cleverly stamped her own creative style in this room, expanding what was once a closet into an extension for a queen-size bed. The antique headboard originated as a wedding gift to her grandparents from her great-grandmother.

The recessed bed is an example of Marcue's decorating ingenuity.

Visitors will find the Inn a convenient and easy walk to downtown Gunnison. The B&B lies along the bus route, providing service to Western State Colorado University as well as nearby Crested Butte and Mt. Crested Butte. For guests who prefer to explore by pedal, guests can borrow one of the inn's bicycles.

Expect a gourmet touch for breakfast, with enticing fare like Greek yogurt with fresh fruit, almonds, kasha and cinnamon. Guests can arrange for other meals upon request.

According to Beth, "Expect to feel at home" at this residential B&B, "but not intruded upon."

PAST AND PRESENT

The Gunnison Valley served as seasonal habitation for Ute tribes for centuries, for trappers and mountain men in the early 1700s, and for exploratory transcontinental railroad routes in the early 1850s. The region began to see permanent residents during the 1870s when miners started staking and working claims.

Topographers began mapping the Gunnison Country in 1874, and the town of Gunnison took shape and grew into a supply center by the late 1870s.

Two railroads competed to reach the area, but the east and west sides of town disagreed about where to situate the depot, splitting the community into East Gunnison and West Gunnison by the time both railroads arrived in 1880. Only the Denver & Rio Grande survived for the next seventy years.

Capt. Louden Mullen, a Civil War veteran-turned-developer, championed West Gunnison's influence and built a hotel, school, opera house, fish hatchery, and park to promote his side of town. His projects also included a church, a stone livery barn, and the foundations of an iron works which never got off the ground.

During Mullen's time in Gunnison, he built his own house in 1883. A later article in Gunnison's *News Champion* in 1945 describes the house: "There is little, but not too much of scrolled trimming, the windows are beautifully arched and chastely decorated (to use the phraseology of the 80s), the gables supported by carved cornices. The eight-room structure is topped by a distinctive iron railing. The large lawn is enclosed by a picket fence, matching the dwelling in color. It is a house which cannot fail to attract the attention of anyone interested in period architecture – a good deal less flamboyant than La Veta, [*an upscale hotel of the same local vintage*] although of somewhat the same inspiration. The grandson, Elmer Mullen, says it was beautifully and lavishly furnished when the Civil War veteran had it completed."

In the years to come, the building would pass through a number of hands, serving many times as a private residence but also at one point as a day-care facility, an antique shop, and even a video rental store.

That home eventually became the Vintage Inn B&B in 2010.

Legends, Stories, and Guest Experiences

Past residents and owners of the current Vintage Inn never kept (or at least never publicly shared) accounts of haunted events on the premises. One former owner of the property, who undertook extensive renovations to the property in the 1970s, claims none of his alterations to the house provoked the sort of supernatural activity typically reported when buildings are disturbed.

He suggests that current paranormal reports may connect to the current owner herself. This could well prove true since spirits residing on the premises seem to have a strong connection to current proprietor Beth Marcue. (See the following section.)

The surrounding community environs certainly hold a fair share of reported paranormal activity.

On Tomichi Avenue (Hwy 50), only a few blocks from the inn, sits Columbine Apartments, formerly the Columbine Hotel. The building's second floor once served as a brothel in Gunnison's frontier days, and former hotel guests as well as current residents have reported seeing the apparition of a woman – legend says she was a murdered prostitute – wandering the central hallway late at night.

A former B&B that operated as the Mary Lawrence Inn (now a private home) also contains long-time reports of the paranormal. Sitting on a residential block in the northern part of the city, this large structure became home to a prominent local family in the middle decades of the Twentieth Century. While growing up in the house, the family's two children, now grown, told us they'd witnessed poltergeist activity on a regular basis as well as sightings of a full-bodied apparition.

And local Western State Colorado University has recurring reports of hauntings in at least three campus buildings.

Generations of students continue to report sightings on the third floor of Roubidoux Hall of the ghost of a man who died of smoke inhalation many years ago. Some students say they've seen his apparition at their bedside at night. Others claim the ghost locks doors from the outside, recreating the same circumstance that trapped him during the fateful fire. Nearby Ute Hall harbors accounts of a shadow figure in the basement known to pass through the wall of an off-limits storage and boiler room, harmless if a bit unnerving to those who've witnessed the apparition. Additional ghostly sightings occur in Taylor Hall, the original structure for the 1900s Normal School.

As for the Vintage Inn, our own experiences there (see the next section) suggest promising opportunities for paranormal interaction.

The original living room is one of the most haunted spaces in the B&B.

Our Personal Experiences

Even though this B&B has no reported history of paranormal activity, to be fair, it's only served the public as an inn since 2010. We went in on a hunch anyway because of the age and appearance.

Our intuitions proved dead on.

Initially, we took EMF readings in the guestroom, ranging from 450-480mG around the bed and 580-590mG throughout the rest of the room. The kitchen hovered in the mid-420s, the hearth room in the 410s, and the front living room in the 450s.

We decided not to further investigate the guestroom because owner Beth believed it was a newer addition to the building. Instead we focused on the original structure, most of which is available to guests during their stay.

In this instance, Beth wanted to assist as a ghost-hunt team member since she, too, was curious to see what we might find. We were glad to invite her along, and she offered a number of personalized questions that made the investigation more interesting.

We began in the heart of the B&B, the hearth room, where we set up our equipment in front of the stove. Almost immediately, our spirit box spirit box produced several EVPs using Beth's name – fine by us. It was, after all, her house and her invisible roommates! When we asked if any unseen presences could tell us who they were, we received clear replies of "No" twice. Then we asked if they had a story to tell, and we got "Alright." But the single-syllable words that followed didn't produce much in the way of coherent responses at first.

We asked how many spirits were present during the session and heard a response of "Five" from two different voices. (Our spirit box produced multiple voices during the time we conducted our investigation.) Later analysis confirmed what we'd heard in real time, but also additional references to Beth as well as the word "Apple" after we asked if they had stories to tell.

Back in real time in the hearth room, we turned on the flashlight and asked for the spirits present to wink or dim the light as another way to communicate. No response. We also conducted an audio-only EVP session, which later yielded nothing.

Beth suggested we move to the front living room because, to her, that room always held a different feel. We again set up our spirit box, camcorder, and flashlight to see what more we could capture. Beth asked if there was anything she could do to make the spirits in the house more comfortable. Her remark only resulted in more references to Beth. So Mark asked if they were happy in this house. Loud and clear in real time, we heard a man's voice say, "Happy." Mark asked for confirmation that the spirit had said "Happy" and received an immediate "Yes." In later analysis, we also captured "good" following that exchange. Audio-only, nothing else.

But the spirits made their strongest showing in the living room through the flashlight, fluttering at first and then dimming twice almost to the point of winking out. We captured these two episodes on video. We thanked them for their interaction and, on later analysis, discovered a voice saying, "You're welcome," through the spirit box.

While there, Beth asked us to conduct readings in her private bedroom, where she kept a dresser that had arrived in Gunnison via her family's covered wagon. We turned on the spirit box and set the flashlight on the dresser. Mark asked for communication through the light, and we heard a voice through the spirit box twice say, "Flashlight." However, the light never winked nor dimmed this time.

In later analysis of the spirit box recordings, we discovered several additions. Mark asked if the spirits present had any questions for Beth. A man's voice repeated, "Question," followed by a woman's voice ten seconds later also saying, "Question." The recording captured Beth's further request to blink the flashlight, but the response was "Hard." We also captured a woman's voice announce, "Say it," about thirty seconds later. We couldn't determine if this spirit addressed the team or some other unseen presence. We've noticed that ghosts sometimes seem to talk to one another while we listen in. We find interesting the theory of longtime paranormal investigator Tim Woolworth that some spirits mentor others in how to communicate through instruments. The "Say it" EVP sounded to us like coaxing.

One final spirit box analysis remark: Mark had asked if anyone in the room had a connection to Beth's family, and a woman's voice promptly replied, "I did."

We were glad we followed our intuition to investigate the Vintage Inn. Beth must be a good innkeeper as well as a good ghostkeeper. All her spirits appeared happy and polite.

Highlights of the Area

Genuine western hospitality greets visitors who come to this recreational paradise. Biking, hiking, skiing, rafting and all things outdoorsy are at your fingertips. But for those who prefer a more cultural exchange, the valley offers plenty of other attractions as well as galleries and performing arts. Ghost towns scattered throughout the area provide plenty of opportunities for exploration.

Gunnison Chamber of Commerce
500 E. Tomichi Ave., Gunnison, CO 81230
(970) 641-1501
gunnison-co.com

Crested Butte/Mt. Crested Butte Chamber of Commerce
601 Elk Ave., Crested Butte, CO 81224
(970) 349-6438
cbchamber.com

Annual Festivals
- Blue Mesa Fishing Tournament – May
- Gunnison Growler Weekend (bike races) – May
- Gunnison River Festival – June
- Cattlemen's Days PRCA Rodeo – July
- Independence Day Celebration – July
- Car Show/Arts & Crafts Festival – August

Cultural/Recreational Opportunities
- Alpine Tunnel Historic District
  13 miles of original Denver, South Park & Pacific rail bed
  East of Gunnison, CO
  (970) 641-0471
  narrowgauge.org/alpine-tunnel/html

- Black Canyon of the Gunnison
  Some of the steepest cliffs and oldest rock in the U.S.
  Gunnison, CO
  (970) 641-2337 (Park Service)
  nps.gov/blca

- Blue Mesa Reservoir
  Largest body of water in Colorado
  Gunnison, CO

(970) 641-2337 (Park Service)
thebluemesa.com

- Crested Butte Mountain Resort
  Alpine skiing
  500 Gothic Rd., Mt. Crested Butte, CO
  (970) 349-2222
  skicb.com

- Curecanti National Recreation Area
  Series of reservoirs along the Gunnison River
  102 Elk Creek, Gunnison, CO
  (970) 641-2337 (Park Service)
  nps.gov/cure

- Dos Rios Golf Club
  High-country golfing
  501 Camino Del Rio, Gunnison, CO
  (970) 641-1482
  dosriosgolf.net

- Gunnison Arts Center
  Performing and visual arts
  102 S. Main St., Gunnison, CO
  (970) 641-4029
  gunnisonartscenter.org

- Gunnison Valley Observatory
  Largest public telescope in Colorado
  P.O. Box 1227, Gunnison, CO
  (970) 641-1111
  gunnisonobservatory.org

- Hartman Rocks Recreation Area
  150 acres for outdoor recreation
  Gunnison, CO

(303) 239-3600
blm.gov/co/st/en/fo/gfo/recreation_information/hike-info/hike-trails/hartman/hartmaninfo.html

More
- Gunnison/Crested Butte Tourism
gunnisoncrestedbutte.co

- Colorado Info
coloradoinfo.com/summervacationplanner/gunnison-crestedbutte

Chapter Eight
Norwood

Hotel Norwood

Hotel Norwood

1550 Grand Avenue, Norwood CO 81423
(970) 327-0312
hotel-norwood.com

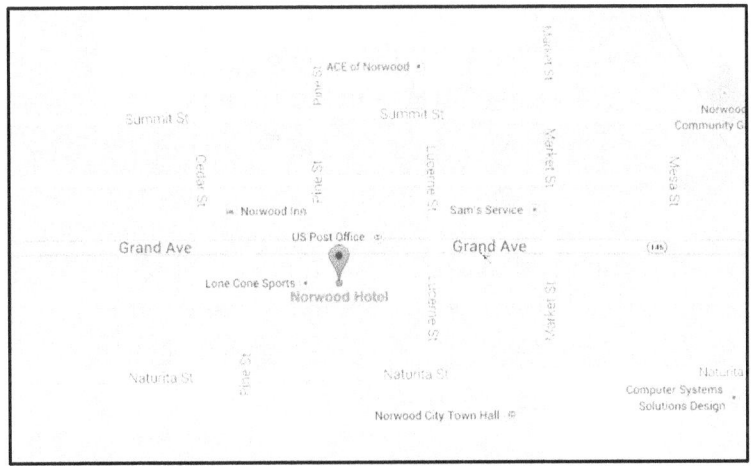

Google Map

Season: Year round
Peak: During fall hunting season (call for dates)
Pet friendly: Only in New Quarters
Family friendly: Yes
WiFi: Yes

Description, Ambience, Furnishings

Motoring in from the east, the drive offers spectacular beauty, skirting the Uncompahgre Mountain Range and passing through San Miguel Canyon. Norwood's location straddles alpine mountains and the sandstone deserts of Utah. Folks who choose this hotel can enjoy the best of both worlds.

The Hotel Norwood, located in the main business district of this quaint little town, looks very different from its 1898 beginnings as the Western Hotel, built next door to the local blacksmith. The exterior clapboard of the original building now sports beige paint with darker green trim. According to staff, past owners expanded the hotel by adding a center structure (with dining room and kitchen) to adjoin the next building, which became the west wing of guestrooms.

The hotel lobby preserves bygone charm.

The key cubbyholes behind the registration desk

The old-fashioned lobby takes on a down-home feeling that (if you're as old as we are) reminds one of a grandparent's house, complete with wooden floor, antique pot-bellied stove, heavy furniture, and old-timey, four-foot-high wainscoting. The entry includes a stamped-metal cash register and a vintage cabinet with individual cubbyholes for keys – things you'll never see in a franchise chain.

The hall off the lobby leads to a dining room walled with rough planking and period furniture. On the opposite side of the lobby, an outdoor patio provides a pleasant venue for people-watching on the main drag as well as tables and chairs for taking lunch *en plein air*.

All guestrooms in the original hotel are on the second floor. Between the fourteen rooms located there and the six rooms in the New Quarters, guests have plenty of options to choose their level of luxury and price range.

We chose to visit only the historical section, where all the paranormal activity takes place. Our favorite rooms were the two suites in the east wing (each with their own baths) and the four rooms in the west wing, which share a bath. All feature antique bed stands and furnishings, and each room offers individual design and atmosphere.

Past and Present

Attempts in the 1870s to settle Wright Mesa east of San Miguel Canyon ran into frequent conflicts with Ute tribes, but in the 1880s, cattle operations persisted and developed on the lush grasslands of the mesa.

In 1886, Henry Copp from Norwood, Missouri, filed on land and decided to name the new locality after his hometown. He built several structures, including a post office, small store, and way station. Within a short time the town began to grow and soon offered three blacksmith shops, several liveries, three pool halls, two saloons, and a bank. The first school followed in 1888 and a sawmill by 1896.

In those days, Norwood mail arrived via packhorse. According to an account in the *Norwood Star* newspaper, "The mail carrier changed horses at Wright's Spring and turned [his] two horses loose to graze. Sometimes it would take him a day or so to find his horses before he could go on with the mail."

Entrepreneur John Davis built the Western Hotel in 1897 (now the Hotel Norwood), which also served as a boarding house. By then, area cowboys frequented the town for liquor, gambling, and prostitutes.

Local historian Howard Greagor recounts that the first automobile came to town in 1909, a Stanley Steamer. Due to the steepness of the grade out of San Miguel Canyon, the water in the automobile boiler wouldn't stay over the fire, so he had to turn it around and drive backwards the entire distance up to the rim.

The Hotel Norwood has operated continuously since its days as the Western Hotel, accommodating many famous guests over the century, including Butch Cassidy and Marie Curie. The facility has operated under a series of different owners through the years, calling the building the Western Hotel, the Back Narrows Inn, and most recently, The Hotel Norwood.

In 1994, owners constructed a new multi-room addition called the New Quarters, remodeled again in 2014 by current owner Logan Tease.

LEGENDS, STORIES, AND GUEST EXPERIENCES

Nearly every staff member we talked to had a ghost story. Most said they have always felt some sort of presence during their work at the hotel but, none of the paranormal activity has ever felt menacing to them. The night clerk said it wasn't unusual for him to hear – or see – anomalous things during his rounds.

Even hotel owner Logan, who lives in the historical building, has heard invisible footsteps coming from empty second-floor rooms above his own quarters.

Room Two harbors paranormal activity.

One housekeeper told us she frequently discovers disheveled bedding after she makes up guestrooms on both the east and west wings of the historic building. She'd recently found a distinct impression of a handprint on the bedspread in Room One on the second-floor east wing – not an uncommon occurrence in this and other rooms in the original hotel.

We had the opportunity to chat with several boarders who'd also gotten used to poltergeist activity in their rooms.

"It's not scary," one of these long-term residents told us. "It's more just little pranks." He said he had repeated malfunctions with his alarm clock and other electrical devices in his room. He'd also had to keep replacing his batteries – a typical reported occurrence for many locales with strong paranormal activity.

Another boarder said he woke up time and again to find his blankets pulled off over the foot of the bed, insisting he was a sound and quiet sleeper. Still another resident had seen a full-bodied apparition in the room across the hall.

Hotchkiss Paranormal Investigators examining the premises in spring 2014 reported finding considerable activity. Their EMF meter, thermal-imaging camera, and spirit box recorded, in their estimation, clear evidence of ghosts on the premises. In an interview with the *Telluride News*, the team said the place was definitely haunted, and they wanted to return for a follow-up visit.

In our own interview with this team, lead investigator Hector Zeferino told us, "A ghost gave us a tour. We pointed our K2 meter at a photo of a previous owner [Laura Hills] and got an EMF spike. When we went upstairs, we asked where to go and received responses via more meter readings." In the west wing, his team also captured male voices with a spirit box. The thing that most intrigued him about the hotel was all the original antiques: "They collect information of the past and record it for us to find."

Our Personal Experiences

This hotel did not disappoint. Our ghost hunt team this time included bug-and-ghost magnate Egan Kelso, our oldest daughter. She'd experienced multiple paranormal experiences before, making her a good candidate for flushing out ghosts at the hotel.

Hotel owner Logan gave us a tour of the whole facility, pointing out those rooms on the second-floor with reported paranormal activity. During that initial tour, we walked through a cold spot in the west wing's Room Twelve – an early promising start, which made us eager to return there.

Nonetheless, we wanted to be systematic, so we started in the east wing rooms above the lobby. We took a variety of baseline EMF readings, starting with Room One, where the handprint on the bed had occurred; and Room Six, with an account of a guest having his bedcovers pulled down on repeated nights. No meter spikes in those rooms while we were there, so we tried EVP sessions in both, but with no results.

Next we opened the door to Room Two and hadn't taken three steps before a coffee cup tumbled off the table and hit the wall behind it. That event really caught our attention. We'd have dismissed it as vibration from a slamming door, but the nearby door remained open. Kym's EMF meter jumped from 300 to 3,000mG, and both Kym's and Egan's spirit boxes began squawking. Egan's seemed to establish a train of thought, spitting out in rapid succession the words "Follow," "Instinct," "Dining room," "Kitchen," and "Cook." We took that as a cue, packed up our stuff, and headed downstairs to the dining room and kitchen.

Our investigation team members all sensed a tingling presence before the bookshelves in the dining room.

There's nothing scientific about the next observation, but Egan and Kym immediately felt a presence in the room. Egan said the feeling resembled the haunting in our old two-story log cabin (see our introduction). She walked straight toward one corner next to an old bookshelf filled with antique volumes, telling us, "Stand right here." In turn, we both did, and each had the sensation of goose bumps and raised hair. When Egan's spirit box blurted out "kitchen" again, Kym and Egan followed that suggestion while Mark stayed behind to do an audio-only EVP session in the corner, which produced the recording of a whispered voice saying, "Help me." The ghost of former kitchen help, possibly the cook?

In the meantime, Kym and Egan staked out the kitchen, where Egan's spirit box soon announced, "Stay." The room and nearby parking lot were too noisy to try EVPs. Plus the kitchen was so filled with pipes and cooking equipment they decided not to bother with EMF readings because all the metal might artificially skew those measurements.

Since we were right below Room Twelve, we decided to go up a flight and focus on the cold spot we'd noticed earlier.

The team all identified a cold spot in front of the armoire in west-wing Room Twelve.

The cold column of air was still there, in the same spot between the wardrobe armoire and bed, an easily discernable region we could all walk into and out of. No open windows or draft, and the air all around it was much warmer. That's when the conversation really kicked in. We asked the spirit to communicate by turning on a flashlight we placed on the floor in the cold spot. Before long, Egan's spirit box chirped, "Trying" and then, "Practicing," while Kym's EMF meter soared from 300 to 3,560mG and then back to 300mG afterward.

We asked the spirit for a name and immediately got, "Leah." The three of us starting talking about what was happening, but the spirit box announced, "Quiet." The flashlight never turned on. But when Kym asked if we were talking to Leah, the box immediately repeated, "Leah." Our later analysis of the EVP session in that room brought out a woman's voice that said, "Stay," a repeat of the spirit box in the kitchen directly below.

In case Egan didn't know where she was when she stepped into the bathroom next door, her spirit box told her, "Bathroom." This happened right after our visit with Leah.

We experienced strong EMF readings and flashlight interaction in Room Nine.

Our final investigation focused across the stairwell in Room Nine. Within two seconds, Egan's spirit box said, "Flashlight." This time we turned it on and asked the presence in the room to turn it off. With no delay, the light flashed off, then began blinking, and finally diminished the 160-lumen strength to a barely visible glow. At the same time, Kym's EMF meter shot up to an astounding 10,710mG from a baseline of 230mG. Egan's phone battery drained 50 percent during this episode. We tested the flashlight to see if it, too, had drained, but it came back on at full strength. (Later we repeatedly retested the flashlight at home, and it never blinked or dimmed.)

Egan asked the spirit to identify itself, and she got a quick response from her spirit box that said, "Jack." We asked its circumstances, and Mark's spirit box said, "Guess." We also received some clues: "Bush," "Dive," "Alone." We found no audio-only EVPs from Room Nine.

With so many rooms to investigate, we'd decided not to keep setting up and tearing down the camcorder. In retrospect, we wish we had – particularly during the flashlight episode.

We almost felt guilty packing up to leave. The spirit in Room Nine was alone, the one in Room Twelve wanted us to stay, and the cook in the dining room had asked for help. But it was time to go.

Highlights of the Area

Keeping its Old West charm, this little hamlet boasts the best of all worlds: mountain scenery on one side and expansive desert on the other. Surrounding forests and rivers and a nearby reservoir make this an ideal place for hunting, fishing, and water sports. Time stands still in Norwood – but with all the amenities.

Norwood Chamber of Commerce
1525 Grand Ave., Norwood, CO 81423
(970) 327-4928
norwoodcolorado.com

Annual Festivals
- Telluride Mountain Film Festival – May
- Telluride Balloon Festival – June
- Telluride Blue Grass Festival – June
- Telluride Wine Festival – June
- San Miguel Basin Fair & Rodeo – July
- Telluride Yoga Festival – July

- Telluride Jazz Celebration – July/August
- Telluride Mushroom Festival – August
- Sportsman Challenge – September

Cultural/Recreational Opportunities
- Lone Cone State Wildlife Area
  5,000 acres for recreation
  Dolores, CO
  (303) 297-1192
  cpw.state.co.us/swa/Jim%20Olterman%20-%20Lone%20Cone%20SWA

- Miramonte Reservoir
  420-acre reservoir stocked with rainbow trout
  Norwood, CO
  trails.com/tcatalog_trail.aspx?trailid=FGR037-006

- San Juan National Forest
  1.8 million acres for recreation
  15 Burnett Court, Durango, CO
  (970) 247-4874
  fs.usda.gov/sanjuan

- Telluride Ski Resort
  Alpine skiing
  565 Mountain Village Blvd., Telluride, CO
  (800) 778-8581
  tellurideskiresort.com

More
- Colorado's Rio Grande Country
  riograndecountry.com

Chapter Nine
Ouray

Beaumont Hotel & Spa

Beaumont Hotel & Spa

505 Main St, Ouray, CO 81427
(970) 325-7000
beaumonthotel.com

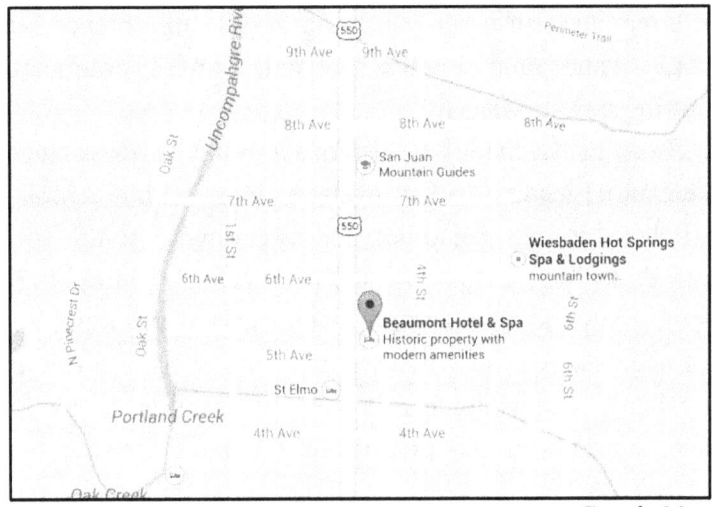

Google Map

Season: Year round
Peak: May to October
Pet friendly: No
Family friendly: Children 16+
WiFi: Yes

DESCRIPTION, AMBIENCE, FURNISHINGS

Mixing yesteryear extravagance and modern convenience, the Beaumont Hotel sits in the narrow valley of downtown Ouray, with towering mountains on all sides. We had no trouble locating the three-story structure, boasting a style that blends Victorian, Queen Anne, and French Second Empire architecture and featuring a slate Mansard roof.

Once inside, the lobby displays a grand staircase (there's also an elevator) leading to two upstairs floors with a central rotunda encircled by two balconies looking down on the lobby and upwards to huge latticed skylights. It reflects Ouray's 1886 gold boom, complete with antique piano, period furniture, and wood trim accents. All the windows and woodwork are original from the 1880s. The wallpaper is new but duplicated by the same manufacturer (still in operation) for the initial construction.

The lobby retains the elegance of Ouray's 1880s heyday.

Off the lobby, guests can visit an adjoining bookstore, accessible from the street and open year round.

Co-owner Jennifer Leaver refers to the facility as a "boutique hotel" because of its amenities and lavish design. Her tour of the hotel revealed a spa suite that offers separate rooms for massage, reflexology, hot tub and sauna, and therapeutic treatments. Off the lobby, the Beaumont Grill has replaced the hotel's old melodrama theater and specializes in American-style cuisine and wine (one of the Western Slope's largest wine collections). One impressive room occupies virtually half the second floor – the rosewood grand ballroom, a 21-foot-high space reserved for weddings, seasonal parties, and other special occasions. Down the hall, Luella's Lounge offers an extra space for relaxing.

The rosewood trim in the Grand Ballroom continues a tradition of catering parties.

Each of the twelve guestrooms, including the Tower Suite, follows an individual design, variously including Tiffany chandeliers, four-poster beds, armoires, and lavish private baths. Guests can choose from rooms and suites containing king and queen beds, with such features as marble vanities, claw-foot bathtubs, and skylights.

Past and Present

The San Juan range is one of the most highly mineralized sections in Colorado, drawing miners to Ouray as early as the 1850s in search of silver and gold, although the serious rush began in the 1870s. The area's mining heyday peaked for a decade starting in 1883. Horses, burros, mules, and carriages brought the first prospectors, and the population began to soar with reported silver strikes. The railroad made it to the valley in 1891, and Ouray grew from a miners' camp to a flourishing frontier community. Queen Anne Victorian storefronts and hotels popped up throughout the fledgling town, including the Beaumont Hotel, built in 1886 of bricks fired from the mud of local hot springs.

The hotel began as an enterprise to entertain railroad and mining investors to the area and claims the distinction as one of the first in the country wired for AC current. Like many Old West towns, soiled doves frequented the local lodging establishments. A private staircase at the Beaumont provided "unescorted ladies" access to their clients – it still exists, though now used primarily by staff.

The so-called Unescorted Ladies Stairway once gave discreet passage to ladies of the night.

Most mines in the region closed by 1923, followed by the train's closure in 1936. Because of diminishing tourism in this area during the mid-twentieth century, the Beaumont Hotel shut down in 1964. For nearly forty years the building stood vacant and fell into disrepair. The hotel sold in 1998 and new owners remodeled and reconfigured the rooms. After reopening in 2003, the hotel received the Governor's Award for Historic Preservation. A year later, it earned one of the first Preserve America Presidential Awards for historic preservation. Most of Ouray's permanent buildings constructed between 1880-1900 still stand, skillfully restored.

The hotel's lounge is named after Luella Huey, the last known prostitute practicing out of the Beaumont. According to a plaque next to the bar, "As young children, her daughter Judy and her two younger cousins would search for Luella in hopes of finding her entertaining one of her many local miner friends. If the pursuit was successful, each child was rewarded a silver dollar.... If all else failed, the three determined children would climb the staircase of the Beaumont Hotel and gingerly tap on the door of Luella's room. Sometimes their knocks were rewarded – more times not. Years took their toll on the beautiful Luella, and she died at the young age of 40."

At least one murder occurred on the premises through the early years, involving a hotel waitress named Eller Day in 1887. A jealous pastry chef shot her four times in the Luella Lounge. Authorities incarcerated him for a pending trial, but the jail burned down at the hands of enraged vigilantes that very night with the chef still inside.

The Beaumont boasts through the years such famous guests as presidents Theodore Roosevelt and Herbert Hoover, King Leopold of Belgium, Chipeta (widow of Ute Chief Ouray), actresses Sarah Bernhardt, Angie Dickinson and, more recently, Oprah Winfrey.

Current owners Chad and Jennifer Leaver bought the hotel in 2010.

Today, recreationists can enjoy many of the high-country routes that miners developed over a century ago, still leading to nearby ghost towns and abandoned mines.

Legends, Stories, and Guest Experiences

When we asked Jen about the hotel's paranormal hotspots, she seemed hard-pressed to identify any location that didn't hold such reports.

All of the rooms harbor paranormal activity, with doors locking and unlocking on their own. Guests and staff have also detected the smell of perfume and tobacco smoke in every room and all the hallways – even though the entire facility is nonsmoking.

A full-bodied apparition has appeared before the doorway on the far side of this third-floor balcony.

During renovation of the lounge, workers would gather their tools and put them up for the night, locking the door behind them. The next morning, they always found the tools scattered about, thus dubbing the room the "Voodoo Lounge."

We talked to a staffer who began working when the hotel reopened. He said one specific area in the dining room frequently plummeted 23 degrees in a matter of moments. He also reported seeing a figure behind him reflected in the bar mirror out of the corner of his eye. He'd turn around and no one would be there. The experience recurred two or three times a week, and he always had the impression the figure was a woman. Someone working in the spa told him she often found the beauty products displayed on the table by the door transposed to the floor in the exact same arrangement the next morning. The night person regularly received complaints that guestroom door knobs rattled during the night.

Other regular poltergeist activity includes lamps turning on and off and the presence of inexplicable fog in the hallway. One curious event took place during a couple's first night in Room 304. The man offered to draw a bath for his wife in the antique claw-foot bathtub. She declined, saying she'd wait until morning. To their surprise the next day, the tub had filled with water awaiting her.

In a different room, a guest woke up to a "nurse ghost" sitting next to the bed, and another guest witnessed a full-body apparition wearing a long white dress on the third-floor atrium.

One source relates the story of a ghostly woman said to walk the halls at 2:15 a.m. on every quarter of the moon. Some say her husband murdered her, and she continues to look for him. Supposedly the ghostly scene replays, but only with her and not her killer husband.

According to area author MaryJoy Martin, one of her acquaintances had visited the hotel and found her way to a guestroom she'd stayed in years before. She took a photograph of an old picture hanging on the wall and, after developing it, found the reflection of two gentlemen standing in period clothing. The figures had the appearance of people engaged in conversation but stopping just long enough to look her way as she snapped the photo.

"Our ghosts are just pranksters," Jen told us. "None are ever threatening."

OUR PERSONAL EXPERIENCES

Since our on-site visit occurred during off-season, we had access to most of the hotel.

We'd asked Jen which rooms had the most promising paranormal activity to launch our investigation. She recommended we start in Room 304, where the bathtub had previously filled for unsuspecting guests.

Room 304 regularly treats guests to unexplained poltergeist activity.

Before having a chance to set up our equipment, we both caught a whiff of tobacco smoke close to the door of this *unoccupied* room. (Remember, this whole facility is non-smoking.) At first we thought we might have smelled the coffeemaker, but on closer inspection, that wasn't the source. The odor was clearly tobacco. We took a step backwards and neither of us could smell the aroma. We stepped forward and it had disappeared altogether, only to return a moment later. What a promising beginning, and consistent with accounts by other guests and staff throughout the hotel.

We bee-lined toward the infamous bathroom and hovered our EMF reader over the claw-footed tub that had mysteriously filled with water. Baseline readings registered 530mG. The rest of the suite fell in much the same range: 520mG in the bedroom and 560mG over the bed, which had a wooden four-poster frame. Next we set up the camcorder, audio digital recorder, and spirit box. In real time, we heard a number of single-syllable words as well as "Tobacco" and "Smoke." Guess the entities wanted to make sure we didn't miss the aromas they had manifested for our benefit.

We retrieved the flashlight and invited any spirits in the room to use that energy to communicate. Almost immediately, the flashlight flickered multiple times and then almost dimmed out – twice! – which we documented on video. We felt excited by this two-way conversation involving targeted questions and flashlight replies and consider the phenomenon one of the hallmarks of this investigation.

Our later analysis of the audio-only recording gave nothing new, but the spirit box replay revealed "Babble" and "Birthday," followed by a coughing sound (the smoking habit of one of the local ghosts?).

The Beaumont Spa has its share of ghostly visits.

We next set up in the second-floor spa, a whole suite of rooms with EMF ranges of 510-560mG. The foyer seemed the most convenient location to stage our equipment. We'd had such great luck with the flashlight already, we repeated that experiment – but the flashlight refused to turn on at first. Mark stepped into the hallway with the light, and reentered the spa to try again. This time it came on; simultaneously the spirit box announced, "It worked." On our request, the flashlight flickered twice more. And again, the video captured all this.

Later analysis of the spirit box offered nothing additional to our findings, nor did the audio-only session we conducted.

Our final investigation took place in the Luella Lounge, where our EMF registered a fairly steady 520mG throughout. Except when we decided to go for broke by setting up the flashlight once more. This time the light fluttered only slightly, but more impressive during those flickers, the EMF shot up past 970mG. During paranormal investigations, such correlating events suggest the dimming of the light at the same time as the electromagnetic flux confirms a ghost drawing on flashlight energy as a way to manifest or make contact.

Then, without warning, the EMF dropped to baseline. It seemed like the ghosts had gotten bored with us.

In the meantime, we'd left our spirit box running, but heard nothing definitive, then or during later analysis. On the outside chance the spirit or entities had returned, we switched on our audio-only recorder. We didn't have high hopes of capturing anything with the bar's refrigerator humming in the background. Nevertheless, we analyzed the recording when we returned home and found an EVP of "Jim" when we'd asked for a name.

Ghostly smoke aromas, on-request flashlight winks, and a definite EVP – we couldn't have asked for more during this on-site investigation.

Highlights of the Area

Unimaginable views await visitors who choose Ouray as a destination. Dubbed "the Switzerland of America," this locale lives up to its name with a backdrop of ragged mountains for mountaineering and outdoor pursuits. Winter or summer, Ouray offers a variety of pastimes to suit everyone.

Ouray Chamber of Commerce
1230 Main St., Ouray, CO 81427
(800) 228-1876
ouraycolorado.com

Annual Festivals
- Alpine Artist Holiday – August
- Grillin' & Chillin' Brew & Music Festival – August
- High Graders Mining Competition – August
- Mt. Sneffels Marathon Run – August
- Ouray Canyon Festival – August
- San Juan Chamber Music Festival – August
- Ouray County Fair & Rodeo – August/September

- Jeep Jamboree – September
- Oktoberfest – October

Cultural/Recreational Opportunities
- Bachelor-Syracuse Mine
  Mining history, gold panning, other activities
  County Rd. 14, Ouray, CO
  (970) 325-0220
  bachelorsyracusemine.com

- Ouray Alchemist Museum
  Frontier apothecary collection
  533 Main St., Ouray, CO
  (970) 325-4003
  ourayalchemist.com

- Ouray County Museum
  Local history collectables
  420 6th Ave., Ouray, CO
  (970) 325-4576
  ouraycountyhistoricalsociety.org

- Ouray Hot Springs
  Sulfur-free mineral pool open year round
  1220 Main St., Ouray, CO
  (970) 325-7073
  ourayhotsprings.com

- Ouray Ice Park
  Ice climbing and hiking trails
  280 County Rd. 361, Ouray, CO
  (970) 325-4288
  ourayicepark.com

More
- City of Ouray
  cityofouray.com

Chapter Ten
Paonia

Bross Hotel B&B

Bross Hotel Bed & Breakfast

312 Onarga Ave, Paonia, CO 81428
(970) 527-6776
paonia-inn.com

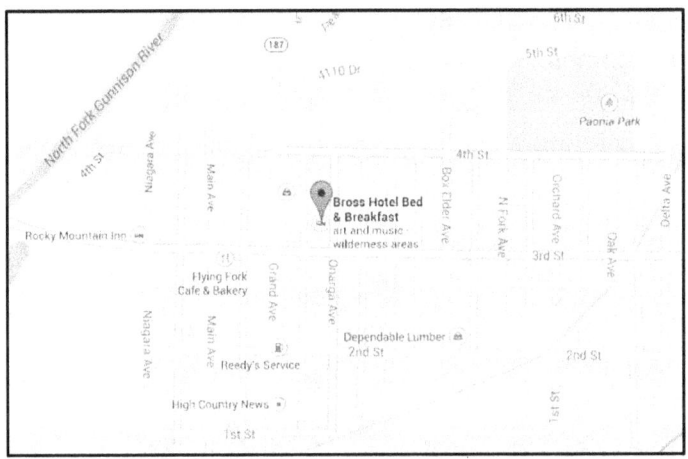

Google Map

Season: Year round
Peak: June, July, August
Pet friendly: No
Family friendly: Yes
WiFi: Yes

Description, Ambience, Furnishings

Approved as a "Distinctive Inn of Colorado," the Bross Hotel is a striking three-story Victorian, charming and well-kept inside and out. The front façade features first- and second-story porches and chairs, with gables and airy bay windows on the sides. The interior combines historic features and modern conveniences. A whitewashed fence encloses a brilliant collection of flowers in the summertime. The back patio includes an immaculate lawn with pleasing settings for clusters of yard furniture.

The B& B maintains a charming backyard setting complete with lawn furniture accented by mountain flowers.

Stairs to the two upper guest floors circle a faux elevator, each floor "stopping" on a different scene from a cold-cast bronze relief called "The Travelers."

Stepping inside the front reception room, the first thing you might notice is a unique door-sized cold-cast bronze wall relief called "The Travelers." The panel depicts a turn-of-the-century businessman and his family – one of four such panels on each floor creating the illusion of an elevator. The open wooden staircase wraps around the faux elevator on all three floors.

The entire reception area is rich with heavy dark wood accents and throw rugs over hardwood floors. Photographs of previous owners line the walls, and old-fashioned looking furniture creates a comfortable seating area. Doorways lead into an adjacent dining room that contains a long service bar, originating from an early day saloon in nearby Aspen. Above the bar hangs a large mirror with an ornate frame. Here guests enjoy homemade breakfasts prepared by gracious owner and innkeeper Linda Lentz.

The hotel's ten guest rooms reside on the second and third floors, each with its own bathroom. The numbering starts with Room Two, the infamous "English/Ghost Room," and runs to Room Eleven. During a 1990s renovation, workers tore down

Room One for the expanded stairway, and the owners decided not to renumber rooms in respect for the hotel ghost.

Each of the guestrooms bears an international name and theme, such as "The Irish Room" or "The Russian Room." Different accommodations provide guests with various sizes and numbers of beds. The rooms are attractive, clean, and spacious.

PAST AND PRESENT

In 1900, William Taylor (W.T.) Bross and his wife Laura Harkness Bross came to Paonia with six children. W.T. bought the lots where the hotel would stand, and in 1905 construction began, using locally fired bricks, still visible both within and without. At the same time, Laura ran an eating and lodging house next door, where the family lived. The hotel opened for business in 1906.

Original innkeepers O.T. and Laura Bross may have passed on, but they still make appearances at the B&B.

The Bross Hotel became a popular lodging and dining facility, and Paonia's *The Newspaper* on April 6, 1906, proclaimed it as "[t]he only really first-class hotel" in Delta county. Triple-brick construction made the building virtually fireproof. The hotel was exceptional for the times, having a basement and three above-ground stories. All floors still display bay windows, attesting to the wealth of the owners. It also contained a furnace rather than a fireplace, indoor plumbing, full bathrooms with hot-and-cold water on each floor, and even electric lights.

W.T. brought guests to the hotel from the evening train, using his horse-drawn cart. Laura, known as Mother Bross, served as the hotel manager, meeting guests at the door, collecting room payments, and explaining the rules of the house. Her granddaughter later recalled that Mother Bross was a "real dressed up lady… in dark skirts, white top, and always white apron. And a black velvet ribbon around her neck."

When W.T died in 1921, their youngest son Otto took charge and retained ownership throughout the 1930s, upgrading and remodeling the facility.

In 1944, Otto sold the hotel to Lura Atkins, but on the condition that he could remain a resident until his death, which occurred in 1959. He wasn't the only longtime boarder. Merrill Henry lived for thirty years at the Bross until his death in 1984.

Through the years, the hotel changed hands eight times. For the past 14 years, Linda Lentz has owned and operated the B&B.

LEGENDS, STORIES, AND GUEST EXPERIENCES

While staying at The Bross, you can pick up an interesting booklet, *Bross Hotel: One Hundred Years, 1906-2006,* written by Linda Lentz, which includes accounts of previous hauntings and apparitions.

In 1993, a family briefly rented the hotel for temporary accommodations. The laundry at that time was located on the second floor, and the family's mother reported she never felt comfortable in that room because it felt like someone was watching her. One day, Mother Bross appeared to her, wearing a black skirt and white blouse. She appeared a second time and the woman tried to communicate with her, but the apparition disappeared.

On another occasion, the children in that family also reported an encounter in the basement with a spirit they felt was a man. They told it to go away and it did. The man in the basement could have been Otto or even Merrill Henry, the other longtime hotel resident.

According to Linda, Mother Bross never really left the premises and has made her presence known in multiple ways through the years. One notable account took place in the late 1990s when a former innkeeper made disparaging remarks about Mother Bross's appearance while looking at the founder's portrait in the reception room: "Immediately, the large mirror over the back bar in the dining room fell down, hit the counter, and landed on the floor without breaking." The innkeeper traveled directly upstairs to Room Two, where she apologized, and the mirror has never fallen since. Linda told us the mirror was moly-bolted to the wall and should not have fallen.

The same former innkeeper also said Mother Bross had a tendency to sit on beds, mussing the covers, moving objects, and playing other tricks.

Ironically, Mother Bross ran the hotel but never lived there; her home was next door. However, her son did reside in Room Two until his death. Linda suggests, "She is happy in Room Two.... Mother Bross probably haunts that room because she's looking out for her baby, Otto."

An invisible "Mother Bross" wrenched this moly-bolted mirror from the wall when a subsequent innkeeper made disparaging remarks about the former owner.

Krystal Leandra of Ghost Girl Diaries investigated the hotel in spring of 2014, and over a period of two days interacted with Laura Bross as well as Otto, his wife, and son Billy, and saw the ghost of W.T. Bross. When lead investigator Hector Zeferino of Hotchkiss Paranormal Investigators visited the hotel during the late summer of 2014, he felt invisible hands in Room Two tuck the covers around the length of his body – a common experience at the B&B. The team reported interactions with both Laura and W.T. Bross. Over a period of two days, they also interacted with Ottgo, his wife, and son Billy as well.

Guests have reported apparitions on second and third floors.

Our Personal Experiences

Our experience at The Bross included several tantalizing anomalies.

We first took baseline EMF readings in the dining room near the infamous mirror (described above). Baseline meter output hovered steadily around 270mG but climbed to over 400mG in field strength near the north end of the mirror frame. Goings and comings in this public space prevented us from recording any useful audio-only EVPs in that area.

We witnessed a fanny print on the bed in Room Two, the "English/Ghost Room." Paranormal reports occur in all rooms.

From there, we headed to the second floor and to Room Two, the English/Ghost Room, or "Otto's room." We began by setting up a video camera on a tripod to record movement. We also shot a number of still photographs with our digital camera – but not for long. Within a few minutes, our new batteries drained, forcing us to replace them. (Rapidly depleting batteries is a common cited phenomenon in haunted locations.)

While the video camera ran, Mark scoped the room with the EMF meter while Kym recorded voices using a spirit box. It soon became apparent that the voice recordings reflected Mark's location in the room. When he stood by the video camera, the spirit box declared, "Videotape" twice; announced, "Film" twice when he started taking photos; and even mentioned, "Fan," while he aimed his camera at the ceiling fan. The spirit box emitted forty words during a fifteen-minute session, including two references to "staircase" (just beyond the open bedroom door), "Bed" twice (the room's largest feature), "Room" twice, "Electric" and "Electricity" (one of the novel features of an early 1900s hotel; see Past and Present above).

We've run the spirit box in some locales with only limited response, but in Room Two the instrument became a chatterbox, with roughly 25 percent of the words specifically describing objects or activity related to the real-time investigation.

The box also mentioned, "Shower," and when we opened the attached bathroom door, the baseline EMF readings of 120mG jumped to 450mG in field strength.

We repeatedly asked if Mother Bross or other entities were present in the room, but we felt no presences, nor did the room feel in any way creepy. Our video recordings yielded no anomalies, and our audio-only attempts at recovering EVPs also turned up nothing. We also detected no temperature fluctuations or cold spots.

The punchline came just before leaving. We packed up and smoothed out the few wrinkles created on the bedspread from our equipment. As we headed downstairs, Linda called out that we should retrieve the tourist literature on the vanity by the bed, and we about-faced and reentered the room. To our surprise, the left side of the bedspread looked crumpled, like someone had been sitting there. In fact, it looked exactly like the print of someone's fanny, and very much in keeping with one former innkeeper's repeated observations in this and other rooms in the hotel. Definitely not the way we left it seconds before.

When we mentioned the disarrayed bed once we retreated downstairs, the owner merely smiled.

Highlights of the Area

A focal point of back roads and trails leading into the forest, Paonia not only attracts outdoor enthusiasts, but it also draws a community of local fine and performing artists.

Paonia Chamber of Commerce
130 Grand Ave., Paonia, CO 81428
(970) 527-3886
paoniachamber.com

Annual Festivals
- Paonia Film Festival – Spring
- Crawford Pioneer Days –June
- West Elks Uncorked – Father's Day Weekend (June)
- Cherry Days – Fourth of July
- West Elks Wine Trail –August
- Mountain Harvest Festival –September

Cultural/Recreational Opportunities
- Blue Sage Center for the Arts
  Gallery, stage, ballroom
  226-228 Grand Ave., Paonia, CO

(970) 527-7243
bluesage.org

- Creamery Art Center
Two stories of art from over sixty artists
165 W Bridge St., Hotchkiss, CO
(970) 872-4848
creameryartscenter.org

- Glennie Coombe Gallery
Fine art by Colorado artists
140 Grand Ave., Paonia, CO
(970) 527-6622
glenniecoombegallery.com

- Overland Reservoir
Fishing for brook and rainbow trout
22 miles north of Paonia
(970) 874-6600
fs.usda.gov/recarea/gmug/recreation/recarea/?recid=75205&actid=42

- Paradise Theater
145-seat venue for film, music, live entertainment
215 Grand Ave., Paonia, CO
(970) 527-6610
paradiseofpaonia.com

More
- Paonia Vacation
paonia.com

Chapter Eleven
South Fork

❦

Spruce Lodge

❦

Spruce Lodge

29431 U.S. 160, South Fork, CO 81154
(719) 873-5605
sprucelodges.com

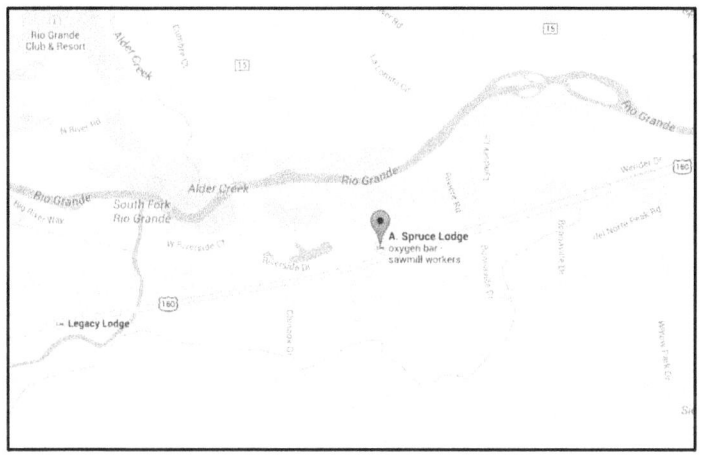

Google Map

Season: Year round
Peak: Only May is quiet
Pet friendly: In cabins and some of chalet rooms
Family friendly: Yes
Wi-Fi: Yes

DESCRIPTION, AMBIENCE, FURNISHINGS

The Spruce Lodge is really a lodging complex, but we'll start with the main building where all the paranormal activity occurs.

The original structure maintains the aura of an early twentieth-century hunting lodge. Its sturdy beams support a walk-out balcony and exterior stairway to a second floor where the boarding rooms of a bygone era now serve as guestrooms. Constructed of chinked logs, the main building opens into a hardwood-floor lobby filled with overstuffed furniture clustered around a woodstove set into a river-rock mantel. The timber theme continues to heavy beams running across the high ceiling as well as in its open staircase above the front desk.

The Spruce Lodge lobby feels like an early 20th Century hunting lodge.

Guests and locals alike gather for breakfast at the lodge.

The ground floor includes a spacious dining room where guests and community members can enjoy breakfast six days a week.

Upstairs, a long shotgun hallway displays antique furniture and easy access to the guestrooms, providing two single-bedroom and two double-bedroom suites, each with flat-screen televisions and electric fireplaces. The suites are large enough to accommodate a family or two couples. One suite even features a Jacuzzi.

The larger lodging complex contains an additional eight chalet units and three cabins. The chalets configure the rooms variously with king and queen beds. Two duplex cabinettes each offer two bedrooms, kitchenettes, full bathrooms, and private covered porches. The larger "Cook's Cabin" comes with a bedroom complete with queen-size canopy bed, a kitchen, and a dining room/living room combo, propane fireplace, and private front porch.

All rooms have private baths, cable TV, refrigerator, microwave, and free continental breakfast.

Twelve RV sites located between the chalets and cabins accommodate all sizes of rigs, with 30-amp service. Pull-through and back-in spaces are available. Sites include electricity, water, sewer, and the lodge complex's cable TV.

Past and Present

As early as 1874, South Fork was a stop along the Rio Grande for the Barlow and Sanderson Stage Company's route, carrying passengers headed to more northerly destinations following the Old Spanish Trail. By 1881, the Denver & Rio Grande Railroad laid tracks through the town on its way to silver mining areas in the mountains further west. The narrow gauge trains served the local emerging sawmill industry in South Fork, and soon sheep and cattle operations as well as farming developed in the Rio Grande valley surrounding the town.

The Galbreath Tie & Timber Company, which began in the 1880s, built what would become the Spruce Lodge's main two-story log structure in the 1920s. The building served as a boarding house for sawmill workers and, except for the hardwood floors, all the wood in the construction comes from locally harvested forests. That mill continued operation until 1999 in what's now a vacant lot across the highway directly south of the lodge.

Although remodeled, the rooms and hallways feature many antiques.

The Spruce later passed into private hands and became a public lodge. It appears on the National Register of Historic Places, administered by the National Park Service as a way to protect sites with historic and cultural significance.

Although one of the oldest communities in Colorado, South Fork didn't become an incorporated town until 1992, making it the "youngest" statutory town in the state.

Rob and Dee Plucinski have owned and operated the Spruce Lodge since April 2006.

LEGENDS, STORIES, AND GUEST EXPERIENCES

The original two-story log building provides the setting for paranormal activity at the lodge, and reports occur in virtually every room of both the main floors and the basement – day and night.

Even before current owners Rob and Dee took possession of the lodge, the previous owners made it clear to expect paranormal events regularly on the premises. Although skeptical at first, the new owners soon discovered for themselves just how haunted their lodge would be, and at all hours. In fact, so much paranormal activity has been reported by the owners, staff, guests, visiting friends and family, and construction workers, we can't mention it all in this section.

Here's a summary, with a few particularly intriguing events in more detail.

These massive antlers in the lobby have twice moved, once 11 inches across this table.

Plenty of footsteps – sometimes for as long as ten or fifteen minutes at a time – occur throughout the building and even within guestrooms while occupied. Owners and visitors frequently hear voices, groans, sighs, and whispers throughout the main lodge. On separate occasions, owner Rob distinctly heard the same woman whisper in his ear, "Look at me" and "Hello." A couple reported hearing Indian drumming in the hallway outside their room, and a plumber working in the basement heard a voice over his shoulder ask, "What are you doing?" while he worked alone.

A whole range of poltergeist activity takes place, including ghostly touches, moving kitchen utensils, rolling balls, moving toys, electrical anomalies, drained batteries, and unscrewed light bulbs. The antlers on the lobby table have twice moved, once eleven inches from its original position.

The Galbraith Room, one of four second-floor suites of the original building where all the paranormal activity occurs

The owner's pets have frequently responded to unseen presences as well.

Apparitions also manifest on the premises. Guests have reported seeing shadow figures dart from room to room or down the second-floor hallway. One building renovator observed a basketball-sized winged object fly out of one room across the hall and into another. No windows were open at the time.

Coming out of the laundry room, Rob noticed a dark figure standing in the doorway to the kitchen, very much resembling a previously deceased owner. He also came face to face with a blonde woman wearing a teal-colored shirt and blue pants sitting on a pool table in the building's basement. There is no pool table in that particular space, but the room did serve as a pool hall in years past. According to Rob, she didn't seem surprised to see him.

Dee had her own encounter with an apparition early one morning: "I reluctantly got out of bed and walked past Rob who was still standing by the alarm clock. I walked into the bathroom and was very surprised to find him in there – not in the bedroom where I had just seen and spoken to him."

Even the owners' children have witnessed ghostly guests. Their son at age three pointed to an upstairs window, asking, "Who dat girl?" The parents saw nothing. Five months later, the little boy told his mother about "the other mommy" who sat on his bed, describing an older woman with white hair and glasses.

Our Personal Experiences

Even though accounts also occur in the basement and ground floor of the lodge, we spent our time in two of the "unoccupied" upstairs guestrooms in the original building. That worked for us, since all the paranormal activity has taken place in the main lodge.

We performed a sweep of the hall and rooms with our EMF

meter, gathering baseline readings: 515mG in the north end of the hallway, and 460 mG in the south. The Baxterville Room ranged from 450-470mG, and the Galbreath ranged from the 330s-360s mG, except the wardrobe which rose to 560mG when we opened the door.

When we returned to the Baxterville Room to start our session, that door had closed – a commonly reported paranormal occurrence at the lodge. We tested the open door at various positions, but it remained stationary.

We began with an EVP session, recording our spirit box interactions, including general queries and our request to dim the flashlight we'd placed on the bed. Nothing happened. Lots of audio feedback and squelching sounds from the spirit box, but nothing intelligible – until we later reduced the interference and analyzed what remained.

That's when we discovered a woman's voice saying, "We'll see," when we asked for the flashlight dimming (in real time, the EMF meter had jumped up 90mG). Also, after asking the spirits to identify themselves, we received immediate spirit box replies of "Hyacinthe," "Betty," and "Frederick." Two other words became clear when we asked who was there: "Kym," who stood in the room, and "Dee," the lodge owner who at the time worked the restaurant below us. Sometimes spirits seem so literal! On the recording, we also heard ourselves arguing whether or not to continue because of the squelching, followed by a woman telling us, "Please talk," and a different woman saying, "Speak."

Mark headed to the Galbreath Room down the hall while Kym packed up the camcorder. For a fleeting moment, she had the impression of a quill pen and inkwell on the table next to the bed. Curious, since the lodge has a reputation for revealing images from a bygone era (see Legends, Stories, and Guest Experiences above).

In the hallway, we'd noticed a mannequin wearing an old-fashioned white nightgown, parasol propped up beside it. We snapped a picture because it looked cool (more on that later).

Once in the Galbreath Room, we didn't encounter the squelch on the spirit box, nor could we hear much else that made sense. But on request, the flashlight did dim about 25 percent, and on later analysis we found the word "flashlight" as a spirit box EVP. We captured this event on camcorder.

We also detected several other words in analysis – "three" (when we'd asked how many were in the room) and "Dagwood." Then came a final name in a voice like nothing we'd heard before, distinct and unmistakable: "DeQuin" (emphasis on the first syllable). It made no sense to us at first until we searched the Internet and discovered DeQuin is both a given and surname of European origin.

On later analysis, we detected no audio-only EVP recordings.

As promised, back to the parasol. After we left the Galbreath Room, we noticed the parasol now lying on the floor next to the mannequin, which stood a mere ten feet from the open guestroom door where we worked. Neither one of us had heard it fall, nor had either of us touched the dress or parasol. Did our footsteps jar it loose? Maybe.

Maybe not. The lodge has a history of physical objects that move inexplicably.

This mannequin stands at the north end of the second-floor hallway. Note the parasol, which was propped against the figure when we arrived but moved to the floor during our investigation.

Highlights of the Area

A high-country outdoor recreation and naturalist paradise, South Fork sits in the shadow of the San Juan Mountains at the confluence of the Rio Grande and its south fork. Travelers can discover a myriad of volcanic formations, geologic wonders, high alpine lakes, meadows of wild flowers, and fall colors for fun all year round.

South Fork Visitor Center
28 Silverthread Ln., South Fork, CO 81154
(800) 571-0881
southfork.org

Monte Vista Chamber of Commerce
947 1st Ave., Monte Vista, CO 81144
(719) 852-2731
monte-vista.org

Annual Festivals
- Independence Day Celebration – July
- Logger Days Festival & Fair – July
- Rock the Rio Grande Rodeo Series – July
- Rhythms on the Rio Grande Music Festival – August

Cultural/Recreational Opportunities
- Great Sand Dunes National Park
  Tallest dunes in America
  11999 Highway 150 Mosca, CO
  (719) 378-6399
  nps.gov/grsa/index.htm

- Mountain Man Rafting
  Rafting tours on the Rio Grande
  30923 W. Highway 160, South Fork, CO
  (719) 873-0188
  theriograndeclub.com

- Penitente Canyon
  Rock climbing
  County Rd. 38A, Del Norte, CO
  (719) 852-5941
  fs.usda.gov/recarea/riogrande/recarea/?recid=64790

- Rio Grande Club
  Award-winning golf club
  0285 Rio Grande Club Tr., South Fork, CO
  (719) 873-1995
  theriograndeclub.com

- Rio Grande National Forest
  5,000 acres for recreation
  1803 W. Highway 160, Monte Vista, CO
  (719) 852-5941
  fs.usda.gov/riogrande

- Wolf Creek Ski Area
  Alpine skiing
  P.O. Box 2800, Pagosa Springs, CO
  (970) 264-5639
  wolfcreekski.com

More
- Colorado's Rio Grande Country
  riograndecountry.com

Chapter Twelve
Twin Lakes

Twin Lakes Inn

Twin Lakes Inn & Restaurant

6435 East State Hwy 82, Twin Lakes, CO 81251
(719) 486-7965
TheTwinLakesInn.com

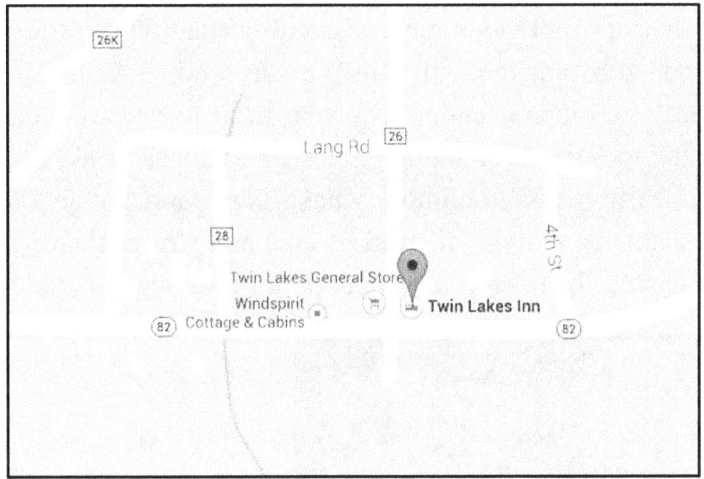

Google Map

Season: May through late September (call for specific dates)
Peak: July and August
Pet friendly: No
Family friendly: 12 and older
WiFi: Yes

DESCRIPTION, AMBIENCE, FURNISHINGS

Before we even arrived at this inn, we felt overwhelmed by the breathtaking scenery of the valley cradled by majestic mountains and two glacier lakes (Colorado's largest). Twin Lakes is a Colorado outpost with only a handful of residents year round, although more live in the surrounding valley. The area appeals to outdoor enthusiasts who want to leave the city lights behind to indulge in hiking (Colorado's highest peak, Mt. Elbert, is a nearby walk-up climb), windsurfing, canoeing and kayaking (available as rentals), as well as lake and stream fishing. During the winter, the town is a destination for cross-country skiers.

Inn amenities include comfy lobby, dining room, lounge, and this breakfast solarium.

The Writers Room: each guestroom is themed at the inn.

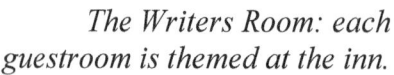

Photo courtesy of Matt Roberts

The inn resembles a Swiss chalet with dark rough-timber planking and decorative forest-green shutters on all the windows and matching trim on the doors. Wooden floors and post-and-beam ceilings throughout the lobby, dining room, and bar as well as heavy furniture – all give the first floor an early 1900s sportsman's feel. We half expected to see Teddy Roosevelt stroll around a corner. A sunny breakfast nook solarium connects the lobby to a full service bar and restaurant, which caters special-occasion dinners with advanced notice. The inn offers breakfast, lunch, and dinner during the hotel season.

The facility offers two public rooms: a library and a wellness room where guests can book massages and hot-stone therapy.

A disability-friendly room on the first floor includes private bath. The other guestrooms contain various configurations of beds, three with private baths and seven without (but the lodge provides bathrobes.) Some of the rooms continue the first-floor motif of wood paneling while others have a more delicate Victorian-style décor.

The two spectacular glacial lakes giving the village its name.

Past and Present

Twin Lakes is filled with Colorado extremes – tallest mountain, largest glacier lakes, one of the worst avalanches, and maybe even its own monster. Read on.

Once a stop along the way between Leadville and Aspen, Twin Lakes was a mining transportation hub during the Colorado Gold Rush starting in 1860.

Built in 1879 by Maggie Webber, the facility that would ultimately become the Twin Lakes Inn once served as a stage stop, a hotel, and even a brothel. A few years later, mining magnate James V. Dexter built the Interlaken Resort across the lake from Twin Lakes, attracting wealthy tourists who boated in the summer and skied in the winter. At one point, a storm sank the connecting ferry, and many passengers drowned. After a dam expanded the lakes and cut off easy access to the resort, interest started to fade and it eventually closed.

An onslaught of tragedy befell the community starting in August 1961, when Twin Lakes suffered a heavy snow storm. Earthquake tremors and strong winds followed in November. Another storm hit that January, accompanied by 70 mph winds. An avalanche struck three days later, killing seven people as the snow freighted at speeds between 150-200 mph and reached the village limits. Rescuers found at least one victim under twelve feet of snow and rubble.

Through tumultuous and prosperous times, the Twin Lakes Inn continued business, even though its name and flavor changed according to each owner. The establishment, in turn, operated under such various names as Twin Peaks Inn, Twin Peaks Hotel, Sportsman's Lodge, Inn of the Black Wolf, and Twin Lakes Nordic Inn.

During the "Black Wolf" era, the owner kept a kennel of

wolves behind the hotel, allowing favorites to frequent the inside of the premises. They usually lay quietly in the dining room. But one day, a waitress dropped a tray of dinners in the vicinity of the wolves. The owner quickly told everyone in the room to freeze while the animals scarfed down the spilled meals. (As far we know, that's the only thing they ate.)

Even though the hotel has undergone several renovations, the town itself has changed very little since its inception. The general store, hotel, blacksmith shop, schoolhouse, and vacation homes of the early miners are still there, now part of the National Historic Register. Even the Red Rooster Tavern and Brothel still remains but currently functions as the village visitor center.

Now a visitors center, the two-story Red Rooster once served as a competing brothel.

Interlaken Lake holds one more secret. According to locals, the waters hide a lake monster affectionately known as "Bessie." If you tire of ghost hunting, you might stroll the banks and keep an eye out for her.

LEGENDS, STORIES, AND GUEST EXPERIENCES

The Twin Lakes Inn has a reputation for guests hearing the invisible footfalls of heavy boots tromping up and down the hallway, and sometimes even the clanking of chains! Housekeeping sometimes finds the impressions of hands and fannies on freshly made beds. Another staff member told us about a music box turning on unexpectedly in the downstairs bar.

A previous owner of the inn once saw an apparition standing in a doorway. She was fluffing pillows in Room Two when she witnessed a cowboy leaning against the doorjamb. She tossed the pillow on the bed, taking her eyes off the figure for only an instant. When she straightened up, the cowboy was gone.

One former innkeeper saw a full-bodied apparition in this doorway to the Mount Elbert Room.

In the mid-1980s, one former guest recounted attending a séance in the second-floor room during a Halloween party. Hands joined in a circle with six others, she witnessed the vision of an apparition coming into the room to accost a shadow woman – *not* one of the attending participants – in a dress printed with pink polka dots. When the session concluded, the guest couldn't wait to share her experience, but the woman sitting next to her spoke first, describing the same scene right down to the dots. Other attendees of the séance also reported the same vision.

Another guest reported seeing a ghost in the upstairs corridor, and still another saw shadowy arms in one of the rooms.

Our Personal Experiences

We focused our investigation on the second floor, where most of the reported paranormal sightings had occurred. The baseline EMF readings for the stairwell were 420-430mG. The main hallway read 440-460mG.

Since the inn had already closed for the season, we had access to all the rooms and recorded baseline assorted EMFs ranging from the low to mid-400s except for three rooms: One, Six, and Ten. So that's where we spent the rest of our time.

We started in "Dora's Room" (Room Ten). A plaque just outside in the hallway described Dora as "a Lady of the Evening," intelligent and refined, who'd worked in that room. To the dismay of the local townspeople, she attended church every Sunday. After a spat with her younger sister Cora, who also worked out of the inn, Dora finally left and plied her trade across the street at another brothel, the Old Red Rooster. That building still stands – although the structure is now a block further west.

Many guestrooms are dedicated to ladies of the night, and we may have contacted "Dora" in her former room.

Attempting to speak to Dora, we had EMF spikes to 550mG, inviting her to communicate with us through both the spirit box and during an audio-only EVP session. The box produced words of a fashion-conscious demeanor: "Gloves" and "Hat" – both suggesting important accessories during her era. Conversely, the box also said, "Resent," "Miss," and "Wreck." Perhaps implying the loss of her worldly life?

In later analysis, our audio-only EVP session in that room did seem to reveal a recreated moment from the past that included what sounded like a sharp report from a gun followed by a woman shouting, "Help!" We never got a clear sense of whether our interaction involved Dora or some other resident spirit.

Across the hall, our next session took place in the "Twin Peaks Room" (Room Six), where our earlier EMF sweep went up to 600mG, and not because of brass bed stands. The room's furnishings were only wooden. Our audio recorder repeatedly shut off when we tried to conduct an EVP session, and Mark's spirit box also locked up almost as soon as we entered – puzzling, since the two devices worked fine both before and after this room. Kym's spirit box managed only a few words: "Listen," "Special," "Fuzzy," and "Sound." When we later reviewed for EVPs, we did *listen* but heard no *sound*, and the track quality was just *fuzzy*!

At that point, we broke off our investigation to walk down the block when we had a chance to interview "Karen" from the inn's housekeeping staff. She's the one who first clued us in about the cowboy apparition. We trekked back to the inn and set up our equipment in the "Mount Elbert Room" (Room One), taking photos and running the camcorder in the doorway where the cowboy had stood. The EMF meter only reached 440mG when we scanned the entire room. However, the spirit box gave us "Speak," "Thirteen," and "Sacrilege." Our audio-only EVP analysis produced a human voice uttering two syllables, but neither of us could make out the words.

Nothing appeared on the camcorder, and no orbs popped up on the photos. But we found two images Mark didn't remember taking – both identical except one contained an odd green streak running vertically at the corner of the brass bed in one of the rooms. Within the green streak appeared what looked like a face with long dark hair.

We enjoyed our time there. The inn has an intriguing history of paranormal activity and deserves further investigation. The spectacular views make it worth returning for another chance to interact with what inn manager Matt Roberts calls the "permanent residents."

Highlights of the Area

This early transportation hub boasts some of the most spectacular scenery in Colorado. Just down the road from Leadville, it's perfect for outdoor enthusiasts who choose to "get away from it all" and embark on fishing, boating, hiking, and bicycling adventures. Winter fun includes snowmobiling, cross-country skiing, and nearby opportunities for alpine skiing.

Leadville & Lake County Chamber of Commerce
809 Harrison Ave., Leadville, CO 81251
(719) 486-3900
leadvilleusa.com

Annual Festivals
- Ski Joring Weekend (Leadville) – March
- Boom Days (Leadville) –August

Cultural/Recreational Opportunities
- Healy House Museum
 Artifacts from a booming silver mining camp
 912 Harrison Ave., Leadville, CO
 (719) 486-0487
 historycolorado.org/museums/healy-house-museum-dexter-cabin

- Leadville Race Series
 100-mile foot and mountain bike races
 Leadville, CO
 (719) 219-9357
 leadvilleraceseries.com

- Matchless Mine
 Rags-to-riches-to-rags story
 710 Harrison Ave, Leadville, CO
 (719) 486-1239
 matchlessmine.com

- Mt. Massive Golf Course
 High-country golfing
 259 Rd. 5, Leadville, CO
 (719) 486-2176
 mtmassivegolf.com

- National Mining Hall of Fame and Museum
 Mining's colorful history
 120 W. 9th St., Leadville, CO
 (719) 486-1229
 mininghalloffame.org

- San Isabel National Forest
 Nineteen of the state's fifty-three Fourteeners
 (719) 539-3591
 fs.usda.gov/psicc

- Ski Cooper
  Alpine skiing
  PO Box 896, Leadville, CO
  (800) 707-6114
  skicooper.com

- Tabor Home Museum
  Home of Horace Tabor
  116 E 5th St., Leadville, CO
  (719) 486-7368
  facebook.com/pages/Tabor-Home-Museum/115978901757827

- Tabor Opera House
  Events and tours
  308 Harrison Ave., Leadville, CO
  (719) 486-8409
  facebook.com/HistoricTaborOperaHouse

More
- Visit Leadville
  visitleadvilleco.com

WILD WEST GHOSTS

Chapter Thirteen

When You Get Back Home

Okay, you've had a great vacation and visited one or more of the hotels described in this book. You've also come away with an assortment of audio and video recordings as well as photos. And you've gotten a taste of how interesting paranormal investigations can be.

What's next?

If the ghost-hunting bug has bitten, the fun's just beginning. As we've noted throughout the individual chapters, our investigations continued once we returned home. The next step is analyzing the data you and your family or team has collected.

What follows are some commonsense tips for going about the next phase of an investigation – plus advice that, we hope, saves you from some of the rookie mistakes we made when we first started.

We'll break the rest of this chapter into the following sections:

- Analyzing your photos
- Analyzing your audio recordings
- Analyzing your video footage
- Uploading and sharing your findings
- Finding other online venues to share your experiences

But first, some advice that applies to all these analysis categories:

Keep your original files separate and protected from those you alter and analyze.

You always want to preserve the raw data, so no one can accuse you of making up files or documentation. That's the first rule of legitimizing your investigations and your findings.

Now let's get to work...

ANALYZING YOUR PHOTOS

➢ Go through each photo and look for anomalies – clouding, blurs, streaks and, of course, orbs or images that weren't part of the original composition of the photo.

Hopefully, you and your team took lots of photos, and with more than one camera. And you labeled each photo, recording a log of the subject, location, date, and time you captured the image, plus any notes you made at the time about each photo.

We've personally accumulated a fair amount of experience as news and magazine photographers, and we're used to taking more photos than we think we'll need or use. As a result, we've also developed a habit of ruthlessly culling our shots in order to keep only the most effective compositions.

Wrong! At least for paranormal investigations.

By prematurely disposing of "imperfect" photos, we found out the hard way that aberrations aren't necessarily operator or camera errors in this line of work. We initially threw away a lot of pictures that may have represented evidence of ghostly tampering as a means of getting our attention.

During our investigation at the Fairplay Hotel, for example, Kym discovered she had multiple pics with blurred streaks, as if she had panned the camera as she snapped the shot. The problem was that the background wasn't blurred. In journalistic mode, she automatically deleted those frames as unusable, not realizing at the time she may have captured more than the obvious subject matter of the composition.

A similar circumstance occurred to Mark when we visited

the Virginia City, Montana, court house. Several pictures taken in the jail contained bright, semi-transparent spheres that Mark at first assumed to be optical aberrations due to the holding cell's harsh overhead lighting. But a number of "bracketing" frames from the same relative camera position captured very similar spheres. Each sphere appeared at different coordinates within the field of view in consecutive frames. Mark had captured a series of orbs! Fortunately, this time we kept the photos.

Another intriguing set of photos occurred at the Twin Lakes Inn, where Mark (using a different camera) discovered two images he didn't remember snapping – particularly since they captured an uninteresting corner of one guestroom that had in no way at the time caught our attention. Like all cameras, of course, this one records and logs photos in the sequence they're taken. The pictures were in sharp focus, but they also occurred at the end of his gallery queue and were included in a sequence unrelated to the Twin Lakes Inn. Mark started to delete the photos, but then he noticed the second depicted a vertical green swath which seemed to contain an elongated figure of a woman. Stretching the image slightly gave that figure even more definition.

A photo we captured but didn't take.

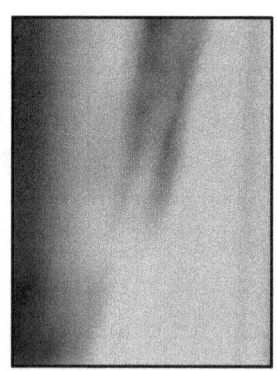

The same photo stretched horizontally.

Did it capture a spirit? The image isn't *that* definitive, but it's suggestive of more than operator or camera error. We saved the image for our files and set it aside as a "maybe." If nothing else, it's intriguing as one more piece of anomalous evidence collected during that investigation.

Our take-away advice: Don't throw away any photos! And make sure multiple sets of eyes examine every picture that team members take.

ANALYZING YOUR AUDIO RECORDINGS

➢ Make a <u>copy</u> of each audio recording and then go to each file to listen for EVPs.

(EVP stands for Electronic Voice Phenomena, those whispers or almost inaudible responses that originate from unseen sources recorded digitally.)

We hope you followed the suggestion we made in the introduction for conducting audio recordings during your visits to the hotels described in this book. We've found such sessions to be some of the most rewarding activities we performed during our own investigations.

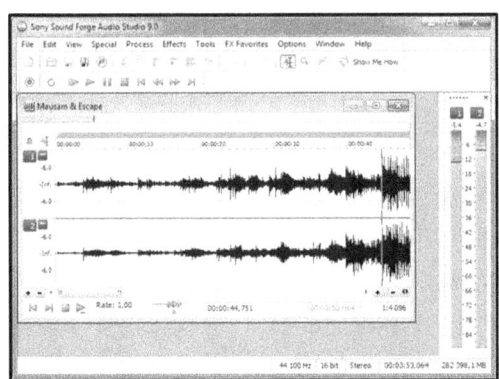

Audio editing software on your computer helps analyze and enhance EVPs you capture.

But the real rewards occur during your analysis of recordings once the on-site, real-time investigation has concluded.

We use two different strategies during our own investigations:

1. Audio-only recordings
2. Spirit box recordings

The audio-only recordings take place during sessions where investigators use a digital recorder to capture questions asked, followed by pauses between questions to allow responses. The theory here is that such responses are so soft that a listener is unlikely to hear EVPs in real time, and only during amplified play-back do investigators discover whether or not the questions receive replies.

Although you can simply play back the recording with the volume turned up, we recommend you transfer the audio files to a computer. That way you can open the files with audio-editing software, allowing you to amplify, slow down, or change the pitch of any anomalies you detect as a means of better understanding what you've captured.

The other advantage of using editing software comes from the ability of observing the time stamps along the way, so it's easier to find and isolate possible EVPs from your raw recordings, opening and pasting these potential responses into new files. This approach allows you to preserve the original in an unaltered form that's available for further analysis.

Recordings of spirit box activity may seem easier to hear in real time, but we often discover things we missed upon close scrutiny during later analysis. We follow the same protocol of transferring these recordings to computer that we use for audio-only analysis. We also manipulate the spirit box recordings, slowing them down and sometimes altering the sounds in other ways to see if we can elicit additional discoveries. This modification proves particularly helpful if your spirit box has an echo effect, which sometimes helps us catch sounds we otherwise miss.

A few words about the bewildering array of effects you can apply to EVPs using audio editing software: Keep in mind that some of these apps weren't necessarily designed for ghost hunting – they're mainly used to edit music files. There's no need to apply the full battery of tools available.

If you've downloaded Audacity (or similar free software), we've found the most useful tools under the dropdown menu called "Effect." We then tinker with various settings under this category with options such as "Normalize," "Amplify," "Change speed," "Change pitch," and "Compressor" – in that order.

It won't take you long to get a feel for how these effects enhance or, in some cases, overly distort what you're trying to hear.

Remember to include enough context in your final files, retaining any pertinent questions you've asked that prompted EVP responses.

Once you're satisfied that you have the clearest sounds possible, you can save your enhanced work as either .wav or .mp3 files. (These formats allow for universal transfer to another computer or device as well as for upload to various Web venues.)

Also, don't become frustrated if you get only meager results. We've captured only a handful of audio-only EVPs in the course of all our investigations. And we've tried to limit the spirit box EVPs we share publically to ones all team members agree on.

Some types of spirit boxes scan radio frequencies as a source of words that spirits can use to communicate. Be prepared for a lot of random single-syllable or single-word utterances if you use an EchoVox, Spotted:Ghosts Spirit Box, or other devices designed to generate random sounds rather than whole words. Just be grateful for any phrases that sound both intelligible and contextually relevant!

ANALYZING YOUR VIDEO FOOTAGE

> ➤ Review a **copy** of each video recording and observe for anomalous images.

Now you're ready to watch your video documentation. It's kind of like home movies of your vacation – but with a twist. Yes, you can relive what you did, but you're also looking for additional evidence of what happened. You might just capture something you didn't realize you had.

Make sure you document investigations so you have more than hearsay evidence.

The purpose of recording video during a paranormal investigation usually takes one of two forms:

1. Static placement to cover an area other than your current location
2. Documentation of your own real-time sessions.

We've tried both approaches – even though we used only one camcorder with tripod for the locations in this book. (As we mentioned in the introduction, we tried to follow procedures that would mimic minimal equipment requirements for those who use this book for their own haunted hotel visits.)

Throughout our investigations, we followed the common procedural rule of two or three team members working together at all times. At first we used the camcorder in a static placement to record a different location from the one where we conducted some aspect of our investigation. This works fine if you remember to use a separate recorder to document what you're doing elsewhere. But it also eats up a lot of memory on smaller hand-held devices.

More important, however, is to make sure you document your real-time sessions. When we investigated the Hotel Norwood, we moved our investigation no fewer than seven times. And we got lazy and didn't set up the camcorder for the last four stops. As a result, we failed to video document one of the more important events during that whole investigation!

If you're using a separate camcorder – highly recommended – these units typically come with software allowing you to transfer raw footage to computer and then edit the clips. For example, our simple digital camcorder came with video editing software, which lets us isolate relevant clips, add transitions, and title words over images. It also retains original sound captured on video but also lets us add audio (generated from our audio-editing files) of our own choosing – for example, if we want to add and replay enhanced EVPs.

Again, remember to work with duplicate files and keep the original raw footage protected.

We've yet to capture anomalous images, ghostly shadows, or independently moving objects on any of our own videos. To be fair, these are rare for any paranormal investigation. But they do occur, and the possibility remains one of the thrills of any anticipated investigation – that, of course, along with a visual sighting of such a paranormal event!

UPLOADING AND SHARING YOUR FINDINGS

➢ Share your documented findings with others in the paranormal community.

We hope you'll consider uploading and sharing your experiences at the hotels and B&Bs included in this book.

Any number of online platforms makes sharing your findings easy. Probably one of the most common, and certainly one that's readily accessible, is YouTube. Another possibility is Vimeo, preferred by many professional video makers.

Our camcorder's accompanying software even came with a feature that uploads directly to YouTube. It's just as easy, however, once you've created a video, to upload directly on your own YouTube page. Don't forget to provide keywords such as "Electronic Voice Phenomenon," "Ghost Hunt," and even the name of the hotel you visited.

We created a specific YouTube playlist and named it "Ghost Hunt Findings" to gather our various documented experiences.

FINDING OTHER ONLINE VENUES TO SHARE YOUR EXPERIENCES

You can link or pin your videos to a site like Pinterest, but there are also lots of sites online specifically interested in your paranormal experiences. Below are a few suggestions, listed alphabetically, to get you started:

ITC Voices (itcvoices.org)

This site, authored by long-time paranormal investigator Tim Woolworth, is devoted to discussions of spirit communication using Instrumental Trans-Communication (ITC) in general and spirit boxes in particular. The articles offer the opportunity to add your own comments (he's very good at responding and including new voices in the conversation), and postings regularly feature the latest technologies and theories behind the ITC phenomenon. He also reviews new devices on the market.

GhostsGhosts (ghostsghosts.com)

Run by Bart DeBlock, GhostsGhosts is a Belgian-based site that features articles and paranormal news from around the world. It also offers links to purchase various ghost hunting equipment.

Google-Plus Communities

Another good place to share your findings are the numerous paranormal communities on Google-Plus. Browse and sample to find one that fits you, and then share in the discussions or post alerts of your own uploaded files on other sites.

Haunted Hour (Twitter @hauntedhour)

A Twitter-based weekly discussion based in London, Haunted Hour has a following from around the world and is a great way to meet up with other amateur and professional paranormal investigators both in our country and abroad. They offer a one-hour interactive weekly chat on Sundays at 10 p.m. GMT (that's 3 p.m. Mountain Standard Time here in Colorado.)

Paranormal Insights (ghosttracker423.blogspot.com)

This blog site, run by Timothy Yohe, offers regular news for all things paranormal and invites the community to participate in the discussions. He also offers an electronic bi-weekly newsletter by email subscription.

Small Town Haunts (facebook.com/smalltownhaunts)

This Missouri-based group of paranormal investigators provides active and eclectic news for all things paranormal across the country but, of course, focusing on the very sorts of places our own book emphasizes – those that are out of the way or off the beaten track.

Spotted: Ghosts (spottedghosts.com)

This site shares videos of documented experiences. Access to viewing is public, but you must create a user account and profile to post links to your own videos.

Write in the Thick of Things

And finally, don't be a stranger! We want to hear about your own visits to haunted hotels and B&Bs, and we'd love to share your stories with our following.

We've set up a Facebook page specifically for your ghostly accounts, photos, and videos at

- Facebook.com/WildWestGhosts

You can also find us any number of ways:

- Website: WriteintheThick.com
- Email: WriteintheThick@gmail.com
- Blog: WriteintheThick.blogspot.com
- Facebook: facebook.com/WriteintheThick
- Twitter: twitter.com/WriteintheThick
- Google+: plus.google.com/+KymnMarkTodd
- YouTube: youtube.com/c/KymnMarkTodd

Most important of all, though, we hope you enjoy the ever-growing community in the world of paranormal investigation!

WILD WEST GHOSTS

Chapter Fourteen
Afterword

We investigated fourteen hotels and B&Bs for this book.

- Did we document real evidence of spirit communication?
- Are we convinced?

We got results – no question about that. But whether or not that's real evidence becomes a matter of both perspective and interpretation.

Even debunker Michael Shermer admits we all live in worlds defined by "belief-dependent reality" – and that's true for skeptics, scientists, and paranormal buffs alike. We each favor evidence that supports the beliefs we hold.

According to at least one famous study, we create our own ghosts. In 1972, mathematician, geneticist, and parapsychologist Dr. A.R.G. Owen gathered an eclectic group of paranormal investigators (none of whom claimed any psychic talent) to perform an experiment that fabricated a ghost they named "Philip Aylesford," a fictitious young aristocratic Englishman living in the 1600s. The researchers initially spent time developing the biographical details for Philip's history, personality, and physical characteristics. Then they concentrated – even meditated – on their personality construct, trying to make their ghost as real as possible for everyone involved in the experiment.

After a year of fruitless attempts to contact their "ghost," the research team decided to duplicate the atmosphere of a classic spiritualist séance. That's when the experiment began to produce results. At first, the communication consisted of rapping sounds on the séance table, but it soon escalated in subsequent sessions to a whole range of other phenomena that defied scientific explanation. Philip started to demonstrate a personality, revealing likes and dislikes and offering his opinions on a variety of subjects. More startling, their fabricated ghost soon proved capable of moving the table, sliding it from side to side, and dancing it on one leg. Philip could even create a cool breeze blowing across the table on request. Sometimes the table became so animated it rushed to meet latecomers and trapped them against a corner of the room. During a television documentary before a group of fifty audience members, the table levitated a half inch off the floor.

But during the final session, one of the researchers explained to Philip that he wasn't real. All paranormal activity vanished. The experiment was over.

Even though Philip was the creation of one group's focused and collective imagination, the experiment raises larger questions about our own abilities to conjure up ghosts. Are we, as investigators – both amateur and professional – capable of exerting more influence than we realize? Can we, in fact, unwittingly fabricate the very ghosts we try to confirm?

We find ourselves of two minds on this notion.

In 70 percent of our investigations for this book, we asked ghosts to manipulate our flashlight. In 60 percent of those sessions, the light did fluctuate. In a good number of the hotels, we arrived expecting nothing. In fact, for several of these locales, we waited to interview witnesses and research historical details after our investigations. Nevertheless, we walked away with 100 percent paranormal activity for the hotels and B&Bs we chose to investigate. In addition to flashlight responses, at the various locations we also witnessed an imprint appearing on a bed, a cup flying off a table, a pillow falling off a bed, a cold spot, invisible footsteps, ghostly touches, EVP audio-only voice recordings, interactive conversations through our spirit box, and several extreme electromagnetic field fluctuations that corresponded to possible paranormal activity.

We repeatedly checked and double-checked our equipment for malfunctions, but our devices only produced results during our investigations and only when we asked for this activity on site. We tried multiple control experiments at home. The result: no response whatsoever.

What's going on?

We've tended to assume these episodes provided evidence of contact with spirits at the investigation locales. Although wary of the unusual success rates we've enjoyed (we know stats for debunking purported haunted locations can run as high as 95 percent), we've tried to take into account that we restricted our visits to haunted hotels with decades – in some instances, over a century – of persistent accounts of paranormal activity from multiple witnesses, many unknown to each other. So we assume our high success rate has some justification. The one exception to these parameters was the Vintage Inn, which had no documented history of the paranormal but where we still recorded results.

We suppose, however, there's a possibility that our findings correlate to the so-called "observer effect" described in quantum mechanical experiments, where observer expectation has proven capable of determining quantum behavior with repeatable, consistent results. Although the absolutely smallest measurement, or Plank level, of activity seems a long way from something as *big* as a flashlight, Masaru Emoto's recent frozen water crystal experiments also prove that human intentions can nonetheless affect the world around us even at the larger molecular level.

Investigators can't dismiss the power of the mind.

But that's the exciting part. Even if we weren't really contacting *ghosts*, could we be influencing the behavior of the light or the other paranormal activity we witnessed? We're skeptical of that as well, of course. We don't consider ourselves particularly psychic – not that we know of, anyway! But we and other investigators could be participating in ways we don't yet understand. Such findings add a whole other dimension to the term "wishful thinking."

On the other hand, we continue our investigations in good faith because some things can't be explained by collective imaginations. Not every instance fits the Philip Aylesford model. Here are three puzzling examples of paranormal occurrences cited from our own book:

- In the Hotel St. Nicholas, we gathered interviews from three separate individuals who'd all seen the same apparition of a tall man in a bowler hat and long coat. None of the witnesses knew of each other's experience until years after the fact.
- Our daughters each saw an apparition at a different time and they, too, didn't share their experiences until years afterward. Comparing notes, they discovered they'd witnessed a figure who matched the same description.
- The three-year-old child who saw the apparition at the Spruce Lodge never had the advantage of joining mental forces with a group intent on creating a ghost. Nor have many other cases of young children who've witnessed spirits. (See "Your Ghost Stories" in the Paranormal Works Cited at the end.)

How can people's experiences, separated by as much as several years, describe the same apparition? And have small children accumulated enough of a cultural frame of reference to come up with independent anomalous stories at such young ages?

We don't claim to have the answers. But every one of us believes in things we can't see. It's part of being human.

Happy hunting!

BIBLIOGRAPHY

The following bibliography groups references and resources by chapter. Following those entries is a separate list of other works we cite for further exploration on the paranormal.

Creede

Alexander Walker. *Colorado's Historic Hotels*. Charleston, S.C.: History Press, 2011.

Clark, Jerry. "Creede, Colorado – A Short History." *The Narrow Gauge Circle: The Denver and Rio Grande Railroad.* http://www.narrowgauge.org/ncmap/excursion7_creede.html

Heller, Leslie. Personal interview. Hotel manager, Creede Hotel. Creede, Colo. 28 March 2015.

"History." Creede Hotel Website. http://www.creedehotel.com/history.htm

"Hotel Man Invades Home…" Account of death of John Zang, original owner of Creede Hotel. http://www.findagrave.com/cgi-bin/fg.cgi?page=gr&GRid=32400230

"Outlaws, Gamblers, and Lawmen in Colorado." Bios for Soapy Smith, Bob Ford, Poker Alice, Calamity. http://www.ellensplace.net/hcg_f12b.html

Toole, M. David. Personal interview. Chef and proprietor, Creede Hotel. Creede, Colo. 28 March 2015.

Crested Butte

Archer, Alexi. Personal interview. Proprietor, Eldo Brewery. Crested Butte, Colo. 08 October 2014.

Barber, Megan. "Crested Butte: The Most Haunted Ski Town in America." http://ski.curbed.com/archives/2013/10/crested-butte-the-most-haunted-ski-town-in-america.php

Crested Butte Museum. Website. http://crestedbuttemuseum.com/

Driscoll, Meghan. Personal interview. Manager, Forest Queen Hotel. Crested Butte, Colo. 08 October 2014.

Florin, Lambert. *Ghost Towns of the Rockies*. New York: Promontory P, 1987.

Gunnison-Crested Butte Tourism Association. Website. http://www.gunnisoncrestedbutte.com/activities.

Sibley, George. *A Crested Butte Primer*. Crested Butte, Colo.: Crested Butte Society, 1972.

Vandenbusche, Duane. *The Gunnison Country*. Gunnison, Colo.: B&B Printers, 1980.

Westerberg, Ann . *Colorado Ghost Tours: Haunted History and Encounters with the Afterlife*. Boulder, Colo.: Johnson Books, 2013.

Cripple Creek

Adelbush, Susan. Personal interview. Owner of Hotel St. Nicholas. Cripple Creek, Colo. 21 October 2014.

Balas, Sofia. Personal interview. Co-owner, Linda Goodman's Miracle Inn (formerly Laset Dollar Inn. Cripple Creek, Colo. 21 October 2014

Barton, Jason. Personal interview. Co-owner, Linda Goodman's Miracle Inn (formerly Laset Dollar Inn. Cripple Creek, Colo. 21 October 2014.

Cripple Creek History. Wikipedia. http://en.wikipedia.org/wiki/Cripple_Creek,_Colorado

Crusha. Shaun. Personal interview. Paranormal investigator. Cripple Creek. 07 March 2015.

Gregg, Chip. "Ghosts at the Lost Dollar Inn." YouTube. https://www.youtube.com/watch?v=vJez9Aa_oBE

Miracle Inn History. Facebook. https://www.facebook.com/LGMiracleInn/info?tab=page_info

Summers, Danny. "More Cripple Creek Ghost Tales." *Pikes Peak Courier*. Online. 24 October 2011. http://pikespeakcourier.net/stories/More-Cripple-Creek-ghost-tales,49678

Tunnicliff, Tom. Telephone interview. Patron at Hotel St. Nicholas. 10 November 2014.

Tuttle, Antoinette. Google+ correspondence. Medium. 16 March 2015.

Del Norte

"Del Norte, Colo." Wikipedia.
http://en.wikipedia.org/wiki/Del_Norte,_Colorado

Rio Grande County Museum and Cultural Center.
http://www.museumtrail.org/RioGrande CountyMuseum.asp

"Town History." Boogies Restaurant.
http://www.boogiesdelnorte.com/town_history.html

Whitehead, Steve. Personal Interview. Co-owner/manager of Windsor Hotel. Del Norte, Colo. 04 November 2014.

Delta

Brand, Annette. "Fairlamb family's roots run deep." *Delta County Independent*. Wednesday, 13 March 2013.

Delta County History. Website.
http://www.deltacountycolorado.com/about/history.aspx

Kettel, Shannon. Telephone Interview. Patron, Fairlamb House B&B. 07 November 2014.

Taylor, John. Personal Interview. Co-owner, Fairlamb House B&B. Delta, Colo. 31 October 2014.

Thompson, Elizabeth. Personal Interview. Co-owner, Fairlamb House B&B. Delta, Colo. 31 October 2014.

Fairplay

Arnold, Lorna. Personal Interview. Owner, Fairplay Hotel. Fairplay, Colo. 04 October 2014.

Fitting, Dale. Personal interview. Owner, Hand Hotel. Fairplay, Colo. 04 October 2014.

Miniclier, Kit. "Fairplay boasts ghosts." *Denver Post*. Saturday, 24 October 1998. 1A.

Pocius, Pat. Telephone interviews. Former owner, Hand Hotel. 17 October 2014, 02 January 2015.

"Rupert Montgomery Sherwood." Obituary. *Eagle Valley Enterprise*. Front page. 23 August 1931.
http://evld.opac.marmot.org/Person/237694

Stanley, Shaun. "Fairplay boasts a host of ghosts." *Denver Post*. Saturday, 24 October 1998. 13A.

Gunnison

Esty, Stan. Telephone interview. Former owner, Vintage Inn B&B building. 10 January 2015.

Marcue, Beth. Personal interview. Owner/proprietor, Vintage Inn B&B. 10 December 2014.

Phillips, John E.. "Capt. Louden Mullin, Promoter, Dreamer." *News Champion*. Gunnison, Colo. Saturday, 04 August 1945.

Vandenbusche, Duane. *The Gunnison Country*. Gunnison, Colo.: B&B Printers, 1980.

Zugelder, Ann. *La Veta Hotel – Its Construction, Operation and Demise*. Gunnison, Colo.: B&B Printers, 1990.

Norwood

Greager, Betty. Telephone interview. Historian, Norwood Historical Society. 17 October 2014.

Greager, Howard. *Smoke: From Old Campfires & Forgotten Trails*. Norwood, Colo.: Greager Howard, 2005.

Tease, Logan. Personal interview. Owner/proprietor, Hotel Norwood. Norwood, Colo. 15 October 2014.

Tuttle, Regan. "Back Narrows Inn may be haunted." *Telluride News*. Online. Tuesday, 14 January 2014. 6:06 a.m. CST. http://telluridenews.com/articles/2014/09/20/norwood_post/doc52d46c0878b41868 943974.txt

Zeferino, Hector. Telephone interview. Co-founder, Hotchkiss Paranormal Society. 24 January 2014.

Ouray

Beaumont Hotel History. Beaumont Website. http://www.beaumonthotel.com/history

Hale, Ryan. Telephone interview. Former staffer, Beaumont Hotel. 20 January 2014.

Leaver, Jennifer. Personal Interview. Co-owner/proprietor, Beaumont Hotel & Spa. Ouray, Colo. 12 November 2014.

Martin, MaryJoy. *Something in the Wind: Spooks, Spirits, and Sprites of San Juan*. Portland, Ore.: WestWinds Press, 2001.

Ouray, Colo., History. Website. http://www.ouraycolorado.com/discover-ouray/history.php

Paonia

Leandra, Krystal. Telephone interview. Co-founder, lead investigator, Ghost Girl Diaries. Denver, Colorado. 10 July 2015.

Lenz, Linda. *Bross Hotel: One Hundred Years, 1906-2006*. Paonia, Colo.: High Country Printing, 2006.

---. Personal Interview. Owner/proprietor, Bross Hotel. Paonia, Colo. 21 June 2014.

North Fork Valley Visitor's Guide. Hotchkiss, Colo.: Over the Hill Media, 2014.

Zeferino, Hector. Personal interview. Co-Founder, Hotchkiss Paranormal Investigators. Cripple Creek, Colorado. 7 March 2015.

South Fork

Carothers, Durrell. Personal interview. Owner/manager, Shaft Restaurant & Bar. South Fork. Colo. 23 October 2014

Plucinski, Dee. Personal interview. Owner/proprietor, Spruce

Lodge. South Fork, Colo. 23 October 2014.

Personal log. Owner/proprietor, Spruce Lodge. South Fork, Colo. 23 October 2014.

South Fork, Colo. "History." http://www.southfork.org/south-fork/history-heritage

South Fork, Colorado. "History of the Area." http://www.southfork.org/south-fork/history-heritage

Twin Lakes

Adkins, Dale. 'A History of Colorado Avalanche Accidents, 1859-2006." Montana State University Archive Library. Bozeman, Mont. http://*arc.lib.montana.edu/snow-science/objects/issw-2006-287-297.pdf*

Chickering, Sharon. "Twin Lakes Tragedy." *Colorado Central Magazine*. 01 January 2000.

Graff, Mark. Personal interview. Co-owner, Twin Lakes Inn. Twin Lakes, Colo. 14 October 2014.

Nash, Doug and Marji. Personal interview. Co-owners, Twin Lakes Inn. Twin Lakes, Colo. 14 October 2014.

Roberts, Matt. Personal interview. General manager and executive chef, Twin Lakes Inn. Twin Lakes, Colo. 14 October 2014.

Schovald, Arlene. Telephone interview. Patron, Twin Lakes Inn. 17 October 2014.

Slater, Carol. Telephone interview. Former owner, Twin Lakes Inn. 10 November 2014.

Twin Lakes. Colorado Vacation Directory. http://www.coloradodirectory.com/leadville/

Wahl, Andy. Personal interview. Bar manager, Twin Lakes Inn. Twin Lakes, Colo. 14 October 2014.

Paranormal Works Cited

Emoto, Masaru. "Frozen Water Crystals." http://www.masaru-emoto.net/english/water-crystal.html

Owen, A.R.G. "The Philip Experiment." YouTube. http://youtu.be/X2lGPT2J1cc

Radcliff, Benjamin. *Scientific Paranormal Investigation: How to Solve Unexplained Mysteries*. Corrales, NM: Rhombus Books, 2010.

Shermer, Michael. *The Believing Brain: From Ghosts and Gods to Politics and Conspiracies: How We Construct Beliefs and Reinforce Them as Truths*. New York: Times Books, 2011.

Wagner, Stephen. "How to Create a Ghost." Paranormal.about.com. http://paranormal.about.com/od/ghosthuntinggeninfo/a/create-a-ghost.htm

Wen, Tiffanie. "Why Do We Believe in Ghosts?" *The Atlantic*. 5 September 2014.

http://www.theatlantic.com/health/archive/2014/09/why-do-people-believe-in-ghosts/379072

Woolworth, Timothy. "Ghost Box ITC at Home: A Note for Beginners." *ITC Voices – Ghost Box Communication with the Dead.* 19 March 2015. http://itcvoices.org/ghost-box-itc-at-home-a-note-for-beginners

---. "Fragmentative and Breakthrough Reception in Ghost Box Communication." *ITC Voices – Ghost Box Communication with the Dead.* 29 August 2014. http://itcvoices.org/fragmentative-breakthrough-reception-ghost-box-communication

Your Ghost Stories. "Apparitions reported by children." http://www.yourghoststories.com/ghost-stories-categories.php?category=18&page=1

ABOUT THE AUTHORS

Mark Todd and Kym O'Connell-Todd are journalists, novelists, and now ghost hunters. They formerly lived in a haunted house for nine years but decided to write about places not quite so close to home.

WILD WEST GHOSTS

www.ingramcontent.com/pod-product-compliance
Lightning Source LLC
Chambersburg PA
CBHW050629300426
44112CB00012B/1714